kisses *of* sunshine

for moms

Other Books in the Kisses of Sunshine Series

Kisses of Sunshine for Grandmas
by Carol Kent and Gracie Malone
Kisses of Sunshine for Sisters
by Carol Kent
Kisses of Sunshine for Teachers
by Carol Kent and Vicki Caruana
Kisses of Sunshine for Women
by Carol Kent and Thelma Wells

carol kent . ellie kay

kisses *of* sunshine

for moms

GRAND RAPIDS, MICHIGAN 49530 USA

ZONDERVAN™

Kisses of Sunshine for Moms
Copyright © 2005 by Speak Up, Inc., and Ellie Kay

Requests for information should be addressed to:
Zondervan, *Grand Rapids, Michigan 49530*

Library of Congress Cataloging-in-Publication Data

Kisses of sunshine for moms / Carol Kent, general editor; [contributors],
    Ellie Kay.
       p. cm.
    Includes bibliographical references.
    ISBN-10: 0-310-24765-9
    ISBN-13: 978-0-310-24765-4
    1. Mothers—Religious life. 2. Mothers—Anecdotes. 3. Christian life—
Meditations. I. Kent, Carol, 1947– II. Kay, Ellie.
BV4529.18.K57 2004
242'.6431—dc22
                                         2004021736

This edition printed on acid-free paper.

Published in association with the literary agency of Alive Communications, Inc., 7680 Goddard Street, Suite 200, Colorado Springs, CO 80920.

Interior design by Tracey Walker

Printed in the United States of America

05 06 07 08 09 10 11 12 /❖ DCI/ 10 9 8 7 6 5 4 3 2

To the children who have made me a mom:
Daniel, Philip, Bethany, Jonathan, Joshua, Missy, and Mandy

ELLIE KAY

. . . .

To Pauline Afman, my mom by birth,
and Rhua Bliss, my mom by marriage.
I love you both!

CAROL KENT

contents

Introduction 10

A Drug-Free Experience, by Ellie Kay 12

Rocka-My-Soul in the Bosom of Mama, by Carol Kent 17

Did I Really Say "Drug Free"? by Ellie Kay 21

My Two Moms, by Carol Van Atta 25

The Funny Farm, by Ellie Kay 29

Shorthanded, by Rozanne Frazee 34

Manners for Moms, by Ellie Kay 38

It's a Boy! by Carol Kent 42

Night and Day, by Ellie Kay 47

My Favorite Storyteller, by Carol Kent 51

What Are You Lookin' At? by Ellie Kay 55

Mom's Mannequin, by Jeanne Zornes 59

Bunny Tales, by Ellie Kay 63

The Wedding Dress, by Pauline Afman 67

Mom on the Run, by Ellie Kay 71

Facing the Fox Fur! by Charlotte Adelsperger 75

Ernest Goes Home to School, by Ellie Kay 78

This Isn't the Life I Signed Up For!
by Jill Lynnele Gregory 83

Growing into His Feet, by Ellie Kay 87

Beaus and Bathtubs, by Bonnie Afman Emmorey 90

Nick News at Night, by Ellie Kay 93

Heart Strings, by Sandi Banks 98

Presidential Appointment, by Ellie Kay. 102

Keeping the Groom — Dumping the Dress,
by Allison L. Shaw. 106

Girls Under Glass, by Ellie Kay 110

Perfect Timing, by Jolanta Hoffmann 114

Things a Dad Can't Do, by Ellie Kay 118

Whining or Shining? by Annetta E. Dellinger 121

What Does Love Look Like? by Ellie Kay 124

A View of the Garden, by Anne Denmark 129

The Stepford Children, by Ellie Kay 132

My Wild, Wacky, Warmhearted Mother-in-Law,
by Carol Kent 136

Girls' Day Jammin' by Jill Lynnele Gregory 140

Mom's Rules, by Ellie Kay. 144

Proud and Prejudiced, by Joy Carlson 148

Money Matters, by Ellie Kay. 152

Military Mom, by Shirley Carter Liechty 156

Chick Flicks and Time Travel, by Ellie Kay 160

Praise Power, by Bonnie Afman Emmorey. 164

Projectiles, by Ellie Kay 168

Mama Needs a Time Out! by Ellie Kay 172

A Tale of Two Manicures, by Jeanne Zornes 176

A Treasure Chest of Memories, by Cathy Gallagher 180

"Mama, I've Got Something to Tell You,"
by Lucinda Secrest McDowell 184

Sharp Shoes! by Diana Pintar 188

Conan, the Barbarian Prophet, by Ellie Kay 192

Who Do You Love? by Ellie Kay 196

A Treasured Letter, by Carol Kent 199

Loser Mom, by Ellie Kay 203

Fast-Food Prayers, by Ellie Kay 206

About Carol Kent, General Editor 209

About Ellie Kay 210

Contributors 211

introduction

This *Kisses of Sunshine* series of five books — one each for moms, sisters, grandmas, teachers, and women — has lighthearted, uplifting, often humorous stories meant to bring a sunburst of joy to your life, as you remember that God loves you. Ellie Kay has joined me in putting these stories together. Our purpose is simply to let God's love so warm and fill you that you become warmth, light, and love to a cold, dark world.

For most of my life I have loved stories. I grew up with a mother who made storytelling a part of everyday life. I realized early on that stories have the power to make us laugh out loud, wipe tears, make choices, and change our attitudes.

Ellie Kay came into my life when she was a new young author, and my immediate thought was: *This woman was born to make a difference!* I liked her immediately and hoped we would be friends forever. She had passion, purpose, enthusiasm, dynamic energy, remarkable creativity, and an ability to find the humor in the most unusual situations. Whenever we're together, I leave encouraged to stand a little taller, to show unconditional love to somebody else, and to take more productive risks that result in furthering the agenda of God's kingdom. As you read her stories, I hope you will not only be convulsing with laughter but will be reading her antics, insights, and adventures out loud to your family members and friends.

In addition to Ellie's obvious talent for writing and speaking, she cares about people and she's an incredible mom who also happens to be trademarked as "America's Family Financial Expert." So get ready for a great read. Her practical advice in these stories can forever change your life for the better. I love this woman.

Sandra Vander Zicht, our editor at Zondervan, has been our inspiration as we've put this project together. Ellie and I want to pay tribute to this gifted woman and let you know that she has been our cheerleader and our coach as this book was birthed.

As the general editor of this book, it has been my privilege to contact many women who have "mom stories" to share. The quality of the stories I received was so outstanding I wanted to double the size of the book. Hats off to the incredible women who shared out of their silly moments, their serious challenges and imperfect choices, and out of their desire to make a difference by telling the truth about the reality of their lives. We aren't all moms, but all of us are daughters. I hope you pass along the wisdom in these stories to every woman you know!

— CAROL KENT, GENERAL EDITOR

a drug-free experience

Ellie Kay

....

*Zig Ziglar says he is such an optimist he would go after Moby Dick
in a rowboat and take the tartar sauce with him.*

JAMES S. HEWETT

I've always been a forward thinker — but sometimes
that gets me into trouble. When I was in my early
twenties, I became interested in what I thought
would be the next stage in my life: having babies. I attended a
small-town church in Texas where several families were into
natural home births. I'd sit for hours listening to moms tell me
why having babies at home was the very best option for Christians. I believed every word. A friend also listened intently and
decided to have her first birth at home, with a midwife and no
drugs.

About the time my friend "Ginger" got to the transition
phase of labor, that final stage before a mom begins to push,
her breathing techniques were not blocking the pain. She

looked at her husband, "George," and said, "I can't believe this hurts so bad — I don't deserve this pain!"

To which her godly Christian husband replied, "You're right, you don't deserve this . . . "

Then he made a horrible, terrible, no good, very bad mistake. He added an ill-timed biblical principle: ". . . what you really deserve is death."

To which his Christian wife replied:

"I'll show you death!"

· ·

When the childbirth season finally arrived for me, I read all the home-birth books, went to Lamaze training, and listened to tapes such as "Supernatural Childbirth." I even considered birthing at home. But by the time the baby was due, another one of the naturalists in our church had almost lost a baby by birthing in her home, an hour from the nearest hospital.

So I compromised.

I decided to be the first mom to deliver a baby in the natural childbirth room in our two-year-old regional hospital. It seemed to be all or nothing in our town: you either used the labor and delivery room or you birthed at home. No one had tried the combination room yet. The student nurses, who were on their OB rotation, were hoping I'd deliver on their shift so they could witness this trivial bit of hospital history. They bustled around the hallway, giving each other an update on my progress. Their experienced supervisor, Nurse Betty, felt my stomach and announced: "I've guessed the weight on a hundred babies, and I've been within six ounces of their actual weight. I'm guessing this will be a good-sized baby of about eight pounds, six ounces." Not only was I destined to make hospital history with this birth, I was going to break Nurse Betty's weight-guessing record.

While I was in labor I concentrated on breathing techniques, and they really worked for me. It was hard, but breathing helped displace the pain — for the most part. However, the closer I got to delivery, the easier it was to get distracted and lose focus. Once, when the door opened, I saw six faces stacked up like a totem pole, all peering in to catch a glimpse of the lady who didn't do drugs. By this time, I felt like a "watched pot" that wasn't boiling soon enough and was not in the mood to be a "class project."

I was also worried about something else. Even though it wasn't my nature to use profanity, I was deathly afraid I would get into transition and then just go crazy and cuss out the pastor's wife who was visiting me in labor. Tip: if you're planning on visiting a woman in your congregation who is in labor, don't count anything she has to say (especially in transition) against her.

After only six hours of labor, I delivered an eleven-pound, twenty-four-inch boy. The nurses dubbed him "Baby Huey." All this without drugs *or* cursing. I know, it's a miracle!

It was such a great experience that I was destined to repeat it four more times. Each was in a natural birthing room and was done without drugs.

I didn't go into the natural childbirth experience with the same attitude as the naturalists from my small-town church. No, I didn't say that birthing a baby without drugs was somehow related to my spirituality. I just decided to try it, and it worked for me. I have scads of friends who take an epidural as soon as they arrive in the hospital. That works for them. They're great moms and good Christians — and they use drugs.

I think most women who have borne children enjoy sharing their childbirth stories — good and bad. Just have any first-time pregnant mom walk into a meeting of Mothers of Preschoolers and ask, "Hey, does anyone want to tell me what it's like to have a baby?" She will be besieged with stories such as:

"I was in labor twenty-eight hours, pushed for ten hours, and ended up having a C-section."

Or: "I thought I was gonna die. I mean, I thought I was going out of my mind it hurt so bad. I just knew I was gonna die."

Or: "I screamed the entire time. I just yelled and yelled and yelled and then I yelled some more."

I'm so grateful I was blessed with good experiences and have encouraging stories to tell. It worked a particular way for me just because it did — not because I was good. Not because I had an extraordinary amount of faith. Not because I'm a naturalist and God honors naturalists. Not any of those reasons. And if you're a tad jealous about my "good story," then just read my "bad story" in chapter 3, and you'll feel much better.

The next time you're talking to a woman who is expecting her first child, think twice about how you tell your "red badge of courage" birth story. Choose your words carefully and try to accentuate the positive. After all, only God knows how a particular labor and delivery will progress and turn out. If you happen to have a harrowing story that could upset or frighten a new mom-to-be, it's a good idea to ask whether or not the woman is really interested in hearing your story. It's important to remember that God cares deeply for every mom in the labor of birth and the labor of life.

. . . .

A word aptly spoken is like apples of gold in settings of silver.

PROVERBS 25:11

rocka-my-soul in the bosom of mama

Carol Kent

All that I am or hope to be, I owe to my angel mother.

ABRAHAM LINCOLN

Some of my earliest memories include the joy of crawling up on my Mama's lap, being hugged to her chest, and rocked until I was comforted, assured of her love, and unafraid.

My mother came from Dutch roots and I loved hearing the story of how my grandfather came to the United States on a big boat from The Netherlands. He met and married a Dutch lady from New Jersey. They settled in Grand Rapids, Michigan, and raised eleven children — count them — that's one short of a dozen! My mother was child number nine and her name was Pauline Wielhouwer (pronounced "wheel-how-er").

Mama had five sisters, and all of the Wielhouwer women had one thing in common — ample bosoms. My aunts had enough love to splash all over any child who came within an arm's reach, and since there were almost fifty cousins on that side of the family, reunions always meant there would be lots of hugging. One by one our sweet aunts would swoop us up into their arms and give us big ole bear hugs. Some of those hugs were so gigantic you could almost suffocate trying to come up for air out of the deep crevices of those well-endowed chests. However, one thing was certain: I always knew I was loved — deeply, completely, and unconditionally.

As I approached puberty, I became fixated on my lack of development in the area of carrying on the family tradition of "ample bosoms." Mine seemed to be very lacking when compared to my female relatives, and at one time I wondered if I had been adopted. I was definitely not developing into the image of the voluptuous woman I had hoped to become.

I was the oldest in the family and, over time, Mama gave birth to her sixth child. During my formative years, there was almost always a baby in the house. Mama believed in breast-feeding those babies, so every time another child came along, I was keenly aware of my mother's engorged breasts and my teeny, tiny "chest bumps." The years were passing, and I finally became a "woman" soon after my thirteenth birthday — later than any of my friends. I thought: *No wonder I'm so underdeveloped. I'm late with everything that has to do with the human body.*

One afternoon I was home alone and I walked into my mother's bedroom. There on the vanity table I spotted Mama's breast pump. It was an intriguing piece of equipment. It had a spherical ball on one end that was connected to a plastic contraption that went over the breast in order to express milk. In my well-developed imagination I envisioned that this remarkable apparatus might have more than one purpose.

Carefully removing my blouse, I unhooked my brassiere (which was hardly necessary for support). I cautiously squeezed the ball, expelling much of the air inside, and placed the other end of the breast pump over one of my own less-than-bulging protrusions. The result was immediate and impressive. My "chest bump" appeared to be growing before my very eyes. Perhaps I was in the process of becoming one of the "Wielhouwer women" after all. I, too, would follow in the footsteps of my mother and her sisters, one day offering my bosoms of comfort to young children in need of hugs, love, and encouragement. I was becoming a *real* woman!

I soon discovered that in order to have both sides identical, it was important to "shift gears" and work on the other side of my chest with equal gusto. To my dismay, my "enhanced" breast quickly returned to its original size after the device was removed. I followed this procedure every day for nearly a week before I finally gave up on my "Breast Pump Experiment."

Fortunately, when I grew up I discovered that a woman doesn't have to have a large bosom to become a good mother. She simply needs a big heart, a readiness to overlook faults, an ability to show genuine compassion, and a rocking chair that can hold a child and make everything "all better" on a tough day.

I'm a grown woman now, but when I'm in the middle of a personal dilemma, I still run to Mama's arms, and she lovingly pulls me to her chest, strokes my hair, prays for me, and reminds me that love covers a multitude of transgressions. And in my heart I know that everything will be okay.

* * *

Watch what God does, and then you do it, like children who learn proper behavior from their parents. Mostly what God does is love you. Keep company with him and learn a life of love. Observe how Christ loved us. His love was not cautious but extravagant. He didn't love in order to get something from us but to give everything of himself to us. Love like that.

EPHESIANS 5:1–2 MSG

did i *really* say "drug free"?

Ellie Kay

. . . .

*If it was going to be easy to raise kids, it never would have
started with something called "labor."*

ANONYMOUS

My husband Bob says that I run the risk of deceiving the reader if I don't mention our son Jonathan's birth. He was our fourth and hardest childbirth experience even though I was in labor with him for only ninety minutes and he weighed only seven pounds, four ounces. On second thought, the labor probably was so short because it was so intense.

As I said before, I become distracted during childbirth as I approach the transition phase, that final stage of hard labor just before I begin to push. Well, during this particular birth, Bob had turned on Rush Limbaugh's television show and was watching it with great relish. His guffaws could be heard down the hospital hallways, and I know the nurses were talking about "the only man on earth who *really* enjoys his wife's labor and delivery."

Here's Bob's perspective of the incident:

Bob: You're doing great, Ellie, I'm so proud of you.

Ellie: Thanks, beloved, I love you so.

Bob: I love you too, honey.

Ellie: This labor is getting kind of intense.

Bob: I'm so glad they have this TV in here. I turned it on to distract you from the pain because I love you so very much.

Ellie: You're such a wonderful husband. But this labor is getting intense. Now I know why women take drugs.

Bob: You've really got this childbirth thing down, honey. You don't need any drugs. I know you really don't want them.

Ellie: I think maybe I do.

That was how *he* said it went. Now listen to *my* perspective, the *real* behind-the-scenes view of what happened during Jonathan's birth. (Note how the guy's version is always shorter than the real version.)

Bob: Wow! Look at this, beloved! What a nice television set. If you can hold off just a bit longer, I can see almost all of the *Rush Limbaugh Show*.

Ellie: You're turning on the television in the middle of my labor?

Bob: Why not? I hardly ever get to see his show. Besides that, this childbirth thing could take a long time, and you've got it down pat anyway.

(Thirty minutes later, and I'm now in transition.)

Ellie: Bob, help! (I was having contractions so close together I could only say a few words at a time between them.)

Bob: (Laughing at the television) Hey, honey! This is really a fall-down-funny show!

Ellie: (I was finishing a contraction and thinking, *You are going to be falling down if you don't turn that thing off!*)

Bob: (By now, he's rubbing the lampshade, thinking it's my arm.) Can you believe that photo of Hillary? Rush is going to take some hits for that.

Ellie: I know someone who's gonna get hit and soon!

Bob: It's time for a commercial. How are you doing, beloved?

Ellie: (An intense contraction was ending, and I could only gasp out three words.) "GET ME DRUGS!"

Bob: (He had a gleam in his eye as if he were making a patriotic speech.) Beloved, I shan't. I shall not get you drugs. You would hate yourself in the morning if I asked them to get you drugs, and I know you don't need them. (The commercial break was now over and he went back to the land of make-believe.)

Ellie: (In the middle of another heavy contraction. I couldn't talk, I could only think, *Buddy, if I ever get out of this bed and get to you, you're gonna need lots of drugs.*)

Jonathan was born ten minutes later . . . just as the show ended.

Distractions can be good or bad, depending on the circumstances. Some, like Bob watching the *Rush Limbaugh Show*, are simply ill-timed. Others, such as watching a funny movie when we have the blues, are good. Still others, such as a toddler distracting you from a phone call, are frustrating. Sometimes we just want to run away from our distractions. That's when it's great to know God never gets distracted. He doesn't put us on "hold" until the end of his favorite TV program; there's never a problem too big or too small for him. When we apply the calming effects of God's complete and undivided attention, then we get through with his help. (But drugs can still be helpful in childbirth!)

Cast all your anxiety on him because he cares for you.

1 PETER 5:7

my two moms

Carol Van Atta

....

Home is a place of welcoming love, nonjudgmental acceptance, kisses, and hospitality — elements that induce a profound sense of belonging.

BRENNAN MANNING

*H*appy anniversary!" the sweet voice chimed.

I rubbed my eyes, attempting to focus on the one person in the world who always loved me — my mother. "Mom . . ." I yawned, stretching. Without looking at the calendar I knew without a doubt what day it was, December 7. Sure, my birthday was November 8, but for Laura Van Atta, this blustery day in December was all that mattered.

In 1964, on December 7, a little girl called Polly was adopted into the Van Atta family, where she was renamed Carol. Every year, no matter what was going on in my life, my mom would celebrate the day she brought me home from the children's center and into her home and her heart forever. On this particular anniversary, at age twenty-eight, I was in her home on my special day, and I wanted to hear "The Story of Me" one more time.

"Please, tell me again. Why me? Why did you choose me?" I pushed myself up and leaned against her small frame, which for me, a tall five-foot, nine-inch woman, seemed extremely small.

"Oh, honey, we knew you were the one. There were two older children there and other babies, but when we saw you, just four weeks old, in your little lace dress, you just looked up at us with those big brown eyes, and we knew you were a special little girl, *our* special girl." She smiled while her eyes misted over, betraying the deeper feelings hidden beneath the surface of her thoughts.

"Even though I've done so many terrible things, are you still glad you picked me?" I asked, knowing the pain and heartache that I had caused my mom over the years — as a rebellious teenager and then as a young adult who had become involved in drugs and other outrageous behaviors.

"Well, I do remember the time you spent the night across the street at Diane's house, and at midnight a friendly policeman found you wandering around." She smiled mischievously. "Or the time you got so mad at me and your father you locked yourself in the bathroom and wouldn't come out."

"Oh, but I did come out, remember? I climbed out the window and knocked on the front door." I had to smile, recalling the look of astonishment on her face.

Then I returned to more serious questions, pain constricting my heart. "Why didn't my birth mom want me?" Although I knew many of the details behind this young woman's decision to give me up for adoption, there was always a rawness that accompanied the joy shared in my family on this special day. Why couldn't I just let go of this illusion of being abandoned and focus on the love right in front of me?

"Carol, I know her choice still hurts you, but I have to believe that God knew exactly what he was doing. I couldn't have children, and your birth mom couldn't keep a child due to her life circumstances. She gave me the greatest gift anyone could ever give, the gift of life — you. Carol, you are my daughter. Yes, I am sad about some of your choices, but nothing, absolutely *nothing* will ever cause me to stop loving you."

As she embraced me, I pondered those words. The truth wrapped itself around my aching heart, refusing to let go. My birth mom, so many years before, had loved me too. She loved me enough to give me life, and enough to let go and release me into the arms of another who could care for me in a way that she couldn't. I had been blessed beyond what I could have ever imagined. I had *two* moms who loved me, not one. Or, as many others in the world, none.

I'm thirty-nine years old now, but my mom still makes sure that wherever I am, whatever I'm doing, she celebrates December 7 — the day she brought me home. And I do mean anywhere! My mom has always had a key to my home, so no matter where I live, she is able to enter at her own risk and deposit my annual "gift of love." I have a whole cabinet of china figurines that reveal her commitment to my special day each year.

Now, as a grown woman, I realize how my moms both demonstrated Christ's love for me. One loved me enough to share; the other loved me enough to never let go. Through these remarkable women, God demonstrated his gift of unconditional love to me.

There are three things that will endure — faith, hope, and love — and the greatest of these is love.

1 Corinthians 13:13 NLT

the funny farm

Ellie Kay

....

Back in Espana, when de mamacitas want to wean a baby who do not want to be weaned, they put the tail of a squirrel into their shirts and when de young child opens his mamacita's blouse — ooooh! A furry tail makes dem no want to eat dere no more!

PAQUITA MACIAS RAWLEIGH (MY MOM)

When I had five babies in seven years and faced the formidable task of being a single mom much of the time (due to Bob's deployment schedule), I knew that I was going to have to practice something my mama always preached: learn to look at life with a sense of humor or you may end up on the funny farm.

My mom is from Spain and should rightly be called *mamacita*. The combination of my Texas drawl and her Spanish accent makes for quite the linguistic challenge. But I didn't always appreciate my mom's accent, no more than my kids appreciate me yelling across the school parking lot, "Now, ya'll don't ferget your permission slips!"

When I was a teen, I went through the "Brady Bunch Syndrome." You remember that, don't you? It's where Jan, the middle girl, was always walking in her sister's shadow. "Marcia, Marcia, Marcia!" Jan bemoaned, "it's always about her!"

During this topsy-turvy time in my teens, I pulled Mom aside and said, "Mom, can I talk to you a moment?"

Paquita replied, "Chure, what do chew want to talk about?"

"Well, Mom, it's about your accent."

"What ax-cent? When I first come to de Chewnited States of Amereeka, I haff an ax-cent. But I no have no ax-cent no more!" she responded with a straight face and a gleam in her eye. She loved to make people smile when she talked.

"I know, Mom, you've really lost a whole lot of your accent. But there are still some words you say wrong. And when I'm around my friends from church, you embarrass me."

"Well, I no embarrass chew for no-thing! Tell me de words and I will prac-teece them!"

"Mom, the other day you told my friend Donna that I cheated on my diet, and not only was I mortified you told her I went off my diet but the way you say the word 'cheat' sounds like a dirty word!"

The rest of the day, as my mom cleaned the house, she was "practicing."

As she dusted the lampshade, cleaned the bathroom mirror, or wiped down a kitchen counter she said, "My daughter, she *sheet* on her diet."

My mom is now in her sixties and things haven't changed much. She knows she makes people chuckle with her snappy accent (which is just as thick as it always was) and her cheerful outlook. She recently decided to look into doing something that would make her look younger. About thirty years ago, someone told her that if she plucked out all her eyebrows, they would grow back fuller and thicker. So she did. But they never grew back — at all. So, all these years, she's had to draw them on with an eyebrow pencil.

She explains the problem like this: "When I was junger, it was okay. I could see just fine. But now, I no see so good. It is hard with my bifocals to see what I doing.

"Some days, I look very surprised!" (When her eyebrows are too high.)

"Other days, I look ver-ry angry!" (When she draws them on too straight.)

"And some days I just look confused!" (When she has one of each.)

So she went to an upscale beauty salon in her neighborhood to see what they would charge for permanent cosmetics that would give her a "happy" look. She entered the salon, went to the front desk, and boldly asked, "Hell-O? Can chew make me look ten jeers junger?"

The receptionist looked baffled and went to get the cosmetic technician, who took an instant liking to my mom and quoted her such a good price for new eyebrows that my feisty *mamacita* replied, "Oooh, that eeese a verrry good price! Tell me, eeese it for one eyebrow — or two?"

The tech laughed out loud and replied, "Well, for you, Paquita, it's a 'buy one–get one free' special!"

. . . .

One of the best gifts my mom gave me was her ability to find humor in any given situation. Her life was not an easy one. Her father was imprisoned for being "on the wrong side" during the Spanish Revolution (the choices were communism or socialism). Consequently, she grew up with a single mom who was quite needy. Then my mom met my dad and left the familiarity of Spain to adapt to a new country, a new culture, and a new life. Although my own mom wasn't perfect (what mother is?), she certainly tried hard to rise above her challenging circumstances, assisted by the buoyancy of humor.

So the next time your toddler takes off his dirty diaper while in his crib and whirls it around the room, the next time you accidentally use Desitin instead of Crest to brush your teeth, or the next time you investigate the sudden "silence" of your child only to discover she's smeared lipstick all over your new bed quilt, do yourself a favor — lighten up, laugh, and lower your expectations for the day. Who knows? Maybe one day *you'll* write a book like this and have other mothers rolling in laughter!

. . . .

*A cheerful heart is good medicine, but a crushed spirit
dries up the bones.*
PROVERBS 17:22

shorthanded

Rozanne Frazee

. . . .

Success is living in such a way that you are using what God has given you — your intellect, abilities, and energy — to reach the purpose He intends for your life.

KATHI HUDSON

Sixteen years ago I was anticipating the birth of my second child. My husband and I already had a three-year-old daughter, so immediately following the delivery when our doctor announced, "It's a boy!" we were elated. A few seconds later, however, my husband looked at this precious infant at the end of the table and saw something that changed his elation to uncertainty. Our baby boy was missing a left hand!

The delivery room was a blur of activity. The nurses worked on our baby as he cried nonstop, and the doctor worked on me. All I could do was lie there, cry, look up at my husband and say, "I'm sorry." I thought I had done something to cause this limb deficiency.

The nurse let my husband hold David for a little while. She then retrieved him from my husband's arms and continued to work on him. Finally I asked if I could hold him. My baby was all bundled up when they placed him in my arms, and I chose to wait until I was in my hospital room alone to look at his arm. I was confused, but I wanted to hold my baby close and comfort him, and let him know everything would be all right. I knew we faced challenges, but I loved him instantly.

When we brought our son home from the hospital, we wondered how this major disability would impact his life. Over the next few months, our thoughts were a jumble of unspoken questions:

How would we raise this child in a society that had so many expectations?

How would we raise him with healthy self-esteem?

How could he ever play sports?

What would other children say when he went to school or when he went outside to play?

If he got married, where would he put his wedding ring? Forget the wedding ring! What girl would want to date him when there were so many men out there with two hands?

We named our son David. Now, sixteen years later, we have watched our son grow up without the use of his left hand. We observed him at age four learn to tie his shoes — about a year or two before most children accomplish that feat. When he turned five, we did what any good parents of a kid with only one hand would do — we signed him up to play soccer.

It wasn't too long before he wanted to play baseball. We looked at each other and said, "How in the world will he do *that*?" But we decided to let him try because at that time one of the major league pitchers for the New York Yankees was a one-handed man named Jim Abbott. David consistently got on base, hitting many doubles and triples. After playing for several years, he became the starting first baseman and pitcher for his team. He also played basketball and, to our surprise, he was one of the highest scoring members of the team.

When David entered junior high school, he wanted to play football. My husband and I looked at each other again and said, "I don't know about this, but he's done everything else, why not let him try?" And he did. In fact, he did *very* well. David has been playing varsity football since his freshman year of high school. He has played offense and defense. In his sophomore year he made two interception touchdowns and this coming year, his junior year, he will play starting quarterback on his team. He has also earned a second-degree black belt in karate.

I look at my son in amazement. He has accomplished more with one hand than his dad and I together have done with four. Looking back, I smile about my concerns regarding dating. David has had many different girlfriends since he was in the sixth grade. This mother is no longer worried about how he will one day find a place for a wedding ring.

A couple of weeks ago my tall, handsome sixteen-year-old stood across from me at my kitchen counter and asked, "Mom, when I was born, would you and Dad have given me one of *your* hands if you could have?"

Rather surprised by the question, tears welled up in my eyes, and I said, "Yes, David, your dad or I would have given you our left hand if we could have." Chuckling, I added, "I guess an adult hand would have looked pretty funny on your tiny little body, but we would have done it in a minute."

He said, "Mom, I'm so glad you *couldn't* give me your hand."

"Why?"

"Because God has given me everything I need in my life to do what he wants me to do."

Now when I feel overwhelmed by a task or feel like a trial is too big for me to endure, or that I just don't have what it takes, I think about my conversation with David. Like my son, God has given each of us exactly what we need to accomplish the things he wants us to do. We are *never* shorthanded when we add his immeasurable resources to our impossible circumstances.

* * *

For I can do everything with the help of Christ who gives me the strength I need.

PHILIPPIANS 4:13 NLT

manners for moms

Ellie Kay

We cannot always oblige; but we can always speak obligingly.

VOLTAIRE

When Daniel was two and Philip was six months old, they were already being thrown into social environments that required certain protocols. One such event was a family potluck dinner at Bob's flying squadron. The noisy room was filled with jabbering kids and their chatting moms and dads. The children were riding herd together in a section designated as a play area, and the parents were getting caught up on the upcoming social schedule.

I kept a close eye on Daniel and noticed him talking to one of the other pilots. Pretty soon, he came back with a package of peanut butter crackers and proudly held them out to us. He was followed by a pilot who uttered six of the most unsettling words a mother can hear: "Does this child belong to you?"

For a split second I was tempted to excuse myself from the conversation, point to Bob and say, "He belongs to this gentleman."

"Well," replied the pilot, "I've been passing out crackers to the kids for the last hour, and your son is one of the youngest guys I gave them to. He's also the only one who said 'Thank you.'"

Daniel smiled sweetly and proudly repeated, "Tank U."

Whew! Crisis averted, blood pressure back to normal. I thanked this kind man for letting us know we were doing a good job as parents.

If he had only witnessed this same child at dinner last night with spaghetti hanging from his nostrils, then he would have had a balanced picture. Take it from a mama who has wrangled with a few preteens in her time: it's easier to teach good manners while children are young than break bad habits later.

Manners are much more than just saying "please" and "thank you" — they are ways of being kind to and considerate of others. Whether we like it or not, people will judge our children on how they handle themselves around others. A few practical ways to instill these thoughtful values with our children include: opening doors for others, letting others enter or exit an elevator before you, looking people in the eye when you speak, and using good table manners (sans spaghetti in nostrils, of course).

Trying to teach my children manners has made me more mindful of mine. When I'm out running errands with a passel of cranky kids and I'm emotionally spent, it can be tough to show good manners. I have to admit, I don't always succeed in being a model manners mom.

As a matter of fact, I faced this situation last week. When I asked a cashier to check the price on a pair of blue jean shorts that was on sale, she replied, "Oh, don't worry, the register will credit you at the end of the transaction. But even if it doesn't, then you can take it to the customer service desk and get a refund."

In front of my children, I grumpily responded, "But that wastes my time — what ever happened to the idea of getting the order right the first time?" The teenager shrugged her shoulders and smiled halfheartedly.

I glanced at her nametag and saw: Cashier In Training. *Yeah well, you need to go back to Training School, sweetheart,* I thought to myself impatiently. I was running late and decided I'd take her word for it — even though my gut said the receipt would show an $8 overcharge.

When I *finally* paid and received a receipt, there was her error staring back at me as big as Texas — I was right and she was wrong. I turned to Cashier-In-Need-of-More-Training and growled, "I was overcharged $8 — you were wrong. I'll have to make another trip to get the difference — I don't have time for this today!" Then I turned on my heel, gathered my restless bear cubs, and stormed out of the store.

About three steps out the door, the Holy Spirit convicted me with this: "A fool shows his annoyance at once, but a prudent man overlooks an offense." I put the bags in the car, gathered my children together, and walked back into the store to apologize to the cashier.

I must admit that I would much rather be polite in the first place than have to go back and correct my poor manners. But it helps to know that God can use even my failures to teach my kids a valuable lesson. I'm thankful that God is there for me when I fail — ready to offer me a second chance (and a third, and a fourth . . .) All I can say to him is "Tank U."

* *

Fools show their anger at once, but the prudent
ignore an insult.

PROVERBS 12:16 NRSV

it's a boy!

Carol Kent

....

*A young man entered an office in response to a sign:
"Boy Wanted."*

"What kind of boy do you want?" he asked the manager.

*"Why, we want a clean, well-groomed, neat youngster,"
replied the manager, "who is quiet, quick, and obedient."*

*"Phooey!" said the youth disgustedly, turning to leave.
"You don't want a boy; you want a girl!"*

<small>QUOTABLE QUOTATIONS</small>

*a*s a young woman in my early twenties I did what
any woman who is head over heels in love would
do. I married the man of my dreams within two
months after we graduated from college. Neither of us had a
job. We had no money in the bank, but that didn't matter — we
had *love.* I bought a wedding dress off the rack for $100, and
since my Daddy was a preacher, his services were free, so down
the aisle I walked — right into the arms of my knight in shining

armor. Gene and I were convinced that with our strong faith, undergraduate degrees completed, vigorous work ethic, optimistic attitudes, and passionate love for each other, we didn't have a care in the world.

. . . .

It didn't take long for both of us to find teaching jobs, and we decided to wait a few years to start having children so we could pay off our education debts. Four years later the bills were paid, and we thought it was time to start our family. We'd read a couple of books about the best way to conceive a baby, so at the appropriate time the following month we came together for the purpose of fun, intimacy, and fruitfulness. I remember standing on my head for a while following our moment of consummate passion, hoping the right seed of love would make its way into the egg.

I don't know if it was the "standing on my head" part of the process that produced success or if it could have happened a lot easier, but one thing was certain — I was pregnant! Nine months later I was at the hospital with contractions that could compete with third-degree torture in a prison camp. I had decided *not* to take the childbirth classes because during the pregnancy I was busy teaching school and finishing my graduate degree. I figured if a woman could read, she could learn everything about birthin' a baby from a book. Who needed classes? Needless to say, I was *wrong*! I was so unprepared for labor without drugs that I *begged* for gas in the delivery room.

During the final stages of labor and delivery, one of our family slogans was born: "Carol says, 'There is no pain worse than childbirth!'" (To "hear" this slogan properly, you need at least three of my brothers-in-law together in a room with my husband, speaking the words in unison, with a taunting tone and a sing-song mockery.) I've forgiven them because what do *men* know about childbirth?

When that baby finally popped out and the doctor declared, "It's a boy," I was more than surprised. I was from a family of five girls. We *did* have one brother. He had red hair and freckles and was born on Halloween, with a disposition to match. But I figured God knew I was much more prepared to raise a daughter. When we took Jason Paul Kent home from the hospital, I had a lot to learn.

. . . .

Over the next few weeks, months, and years, I could have written a manual for new moms on what I learned about raising a son:

- When changing the diaper of a boy, one must keep the plumbing covered or you receive an unexpected shower. (Yes, I learned this by experience.)
- Boys say the word "Dada" before "Mama," so it's easy to get your feelings hurt when your name is not

called out first. (Perhaps this is true of girls, too, but I'm the mother of an only child, so I can't provide firsthand information on that point.)

- Boys have trouble developing the ability to put the "tr" sound on the front of words when they are learning to talk. They make an "f-f-f-f" sound instead. So if your son's greatest excitement comes when he sees a truck, the mother of the child becomes very embarrassed when her boy repeatedly calls out a four-letter word while pointing to a passing vehicle.

- Boys love worms — dead or alive — and they like to collect them in your favorite Tupperware dishes, which destroys your ability to ever again look at that container in the same way.

- Boys are attracted to water, mud, and slimy green moss, especially when they are dressed up and ready for church a half hour before the car leaves the driveway.

- Boys miss their mommy when she's been away for a few days, and when she returns home, a young son will leap into her arms saying sweet things like, "Oh, Mommy, Mommy, when I saw you right now, it was just like I saw you brand-new!"

- Little boys have favorite polyester blankets that are always the ugliest, most worn-out, faded, and embarrassing "blankies" (due to the knotted balls of fabric that accompany overused favorite things). But if you listen closely, you may overhear a prayer: "Dear Jesus, You're just like my blanket, and I won't ever stop loving you."

. . . .

What I thought would be a burden — being a mommy to a son instead of a daughter — became one of the greatest joys of my life. It brought a never-ending stream of humor, spontaneity, high drama, bandaged knees, and common critters (frogs, beetles, ladybugs, and an occasional garden snake) to my back porch. It also moved me to my knees in prayer — and that was a good thing. The next time *you* hear the doctor say, "It's a boy," *celebrate* that moment and know the best years of your life are in front of you.

. . . .

Jesus said, "Let the little children come to me, and do not hinder them, for the kingdom of heaven belongs to such as these."

MATTHEW 19:14

night and day

Ellie Kay

. . . .

All happy families resemble one another,
each unhappy family is unhappy in its own way.

LEO TOLSTOY

When it comes to helping little ones sleep through the night, young moms are likely to get tons of contradictory advice. I remember some advice passed down from my Spanish grandmother, my Abuela, all the way from Spain. She said, "Back in Espana, when de *mamacitas* want to get de babies to sleep and de babies no want to sleep, they go into a field with de beautiful red poppy flowers and put a flower in de room at night. Den de babies sleep verrry good!"

All I can say is that it was a verrry good thing that I didn't know where the nearest poppy field was when my firstborn had those rough nights because I didn't realize that poppies are the source for opium and even the smell from a large quantity of them can have an opiate effect. No wonder those babies slept

47

through the night "verrry good!" But what about babies that don't sleep so good? What's a mama to do?

This may not be very encouraging, but I didn't figure out the "Night, night, sleep tight, yeah, right!" thing until my last baby was born. And the truth came to me in a *very* unusual way. The kids ranged in age from two to nine and getting them all on the same sleeping schedule was very hard. One night, after they were all asleep, I crept into each of their rooms to kiss them good-night.

When I got to the youngest two boys' room, two-year-old Joshua and three-year-old Jonathan looked so sweet that I had to kiss them and even hug them (which you know is a potential challenge — a kiss may not awaken them, but a hug oftentimes does). Nonetheless, I decided to live dangerously and take the risk.

When I kissed Jonathan, whose nickname is "Sweetpea," he kind of woke up in his sleep and his reflex action was to give me a groggy hug with his chubby arms and a sleepy kiss. It was one of those precious memories I hold in my heart.

Joshua's response was different. When I kissed and hugged "the baby barbarian," he kind of woke up, looked me in the face, burped, then rolled over and passed gas.

This showed me two things: (1) kids can be as different as night and day, and (2) you better watch what nickname you give your children because they will probably live up to their name.

The basic idea that their sleepy-time responses showed me is that their personalities are so ingrained that they are consistent, even in their sleep. And if they are so different in their makeup, then why do we, as parents, sometimes feel we have to treat them all the same? Of course we love them the same. But loving them the same doesn't mean that we approach, discipline, and praise all our kids the same way.

Just because your sister puts her newborn in a cradle next to her bed for the first twelve weeks doesn't mean that's best for your newborn. (Our oldest, Daniel, was eleven pounds at birth and only "fit" in his cradle for two weeks.) One of your toddlers may need to have his hands slapped when he reaches for the electrical outlet for him to get the point. Another child may respond to a loud "Stop!" and not need any reinforcement.

One child may need to cry himself to sleep a few nights before he adjusts to a sleeping schedule, while another may need a few pats on the back in her crib to feel relaxed enough to sleep. Philip loved to snuggle with his blanket and sleep with a pacifier, while Daniel threw off all his covers and didn't suck a thumb, blanket, or anything else. This is why a veteran mom of one child may get confused when the second child arrives and refuses to be just like the older sibling.

I'm reminded that God made us the way he did for a specific reason, and he did the same thing for our children. Since that's the case, then he can also give us the wisdom to know how to "train up a child *in the way* he should go" — each child's own, unique, personalized, specific way.

. . . .

*Teach your children to choose the right path, and when they
are older, they will remain upon it.*

PROVERBS 22:6 NLT

my favorite storyteller

Carol Kent

. . . .

Shared stories build a relational bridge that Jesus can walk across from your heart to others.

RICK WARREN

*M*y mother was the *best* storyteller in the world! She gave birth to five daughters and one son over a seventeen-year time span. During our childhood years one of our favorite activities was to gather in the big old master bedroom and climb up on the king-sized bed and find a place to snuggle close to Mama and ask her to tell us a story. We begged for our favorite stories to be told many times over.

Her eyes twinkled when she told about the adventure of falling in love with our father. The soldiers were coming back from World War II, and during that time period Mama had *seven* marriage proposals. Our eyes bugged out. We all knew our mother was beautiful, but having seven men fall head over heels in love with her was a bit much for us to comprehend.

"Mama, what did you *say* to those men?" we asked with wide-eyed wonder.

"Oh, kids," she replied, "I said 'yes' to every one of them. I really didn't know what true love was at that time in my life."

We must have had looks of horror on our faces because she quickly added, "Well, the soldiers all came home at different times, and then they'd be shipped out again for active duty, and when I was with one soldier, I was sure he was the 'one' for me. Then he would leave and I wasn't so sure, so I'd break up with him and date someone else."

One by one mother eliminated the first six men in her life. It took our tall, handsome father, proposal number seven, to convince her that he was indeed the man she was supposed to marry. Mother said there was a spiritual quality about our father's life that, combined with his zest for life and radiant smile, captured her heart. I found myself looking in the mirror, wondering what I would have looked like had mother married one of the other six men.

Mother told silly stories about her crazy antics with her girlfriends, and we would laugh until we cried. She also read stories to us out of great books, chapter by chapter, sometimes holding us in great suspense until the next day when we would hear, as Paul Harvey says, "the rest of the story." Mama often memorized captivating stories about other people, too. "Old Drunken Tim" was one of her tearjerkers, and we'd get the Kleenex box out and weep every time she dramatically recounted the events leading up to Drunken Tim's encounter with Jesus.

One day as my mother was recounting more of her own life journey, she told us that when she was nineteen, she was afraid to go to sleep at night because if she died in her sleep, she didn't know where she would end up. "That fear," she said, "led me to search for a secure faith in God."

I pondered that story a lot.

One day I was listening to a story on the radio. The program was called "Unshackled," and I heard the dramatic account of someone who made an important choice that turned the rest of his life around. I don't remember the details of that radio drama, but my heart was tender. Through fresh tears I turned to my mother and said, "Mama, I'm such a sinner. Do you think Jesus would come into my heart, too?"

My busy mother stopped what she was doing and reached for her well-worn Bible. At that moment, answering my question was the most important item on her agenda. She put her arm around me as she turned to a Scripture verse and read, "For all have sinned, and come short of the glory of God."* I knew that was true. I was one of those strong-willed children who looked at my parents through the bars of the crib as if to say, "How soon can I get out of here and take control of this household?" Yes, I could identify with being a sinner.

---

* Romans 3:23 KJV.

Mama quickly turned to another verse in her Bible and read, "For the wages of sin is death; but the gift of God is eternal life through Christ Jesus our Lord."* That day my mother told me the most important story I have ever heard. "Carol, God loves you so much that he sent his Son to die for your sin. When Jesus died on the cross he was sinless, and he willingly paid the price for all of your wrongdoing. Three days later he rose again, and today he's preparing a place in heaven for all who believe in him. If you tell Jesus you are sorry for your sin and ask him to come into your life, you will be born into God's family. The best part of the story is that you don't have to be afraid to die because when you leave this earth, you will go to live with Jesus in heaven."

That day a huge burden rolled off my young shoulders. Mama got on her knees next to me, and she listened as I prayed and made the most important choice of my life — to become a Christian. It was a simple, sincere prayer, asking Jesus to be my Savior. And I've been telling that same story to others ever since my mother first told me the most important love story of all.

. . . .

God didn't go to all the trouble of sending his Son merely to point an accusing finger, telling the world how bad it was. He came to help, to put the world right again. Anyone who trusts in him is acquitted.

JOHN 3:17–18 MSG

---

* Romans 6:23 KJV.

what are *you* lookin' at?

Ellie Kay

· ·

A tongue three inches long can kill a man six feet tall.

JAPANESE PROVERB

*B*ob says I get grouchier sooner with every pregnancy. With my first child I didn't start to sport a 'tude until the last two weeks. With the next baby I started getting testy about four weeks before D-day. He says that if we had any more kids, I'd probably be a bear two days after conception.

I think he's wrong.

Okay, I'll admit that *once*, when I was nine months and three weeks pregnant with a ten-and-one-half-pound baby whale, I got a little grumpy when one of Bob's pilot friends asked, "How's the little woman doing?" I was *very* pregnant and looking anything *but* little, and I knew it. I was also taking care of four small children and feeling very tired at the precise moment when the unsuspecting yet condescending pilot asked his stupid question.

Compared to what I *really* wanted to say to him (not to mention *do* to him), I think a case could be made that my response was even somewhat *kind*.

Bob disagrees.

My husband even had the nerve to tell me, "Ellie, it is *never* kind to respond with 'How do you *think* I'm doing?'"

At the time, I thought Bob overreacted.

But he didn't.

I was wrong. I shouldna' done it.

Moms know that having a tired toddler at a grocery store or having a belly full of baby while trying to get up from an overstuffed couch can make *anyone* bad-tempered. What our husbands simply do not understand is that we are entitled to act this way. It's all a matter of perspective. But how is a guy to understand?

I always wanted to leave the kids with Bob when they all had chicken pox and go shopping with a girlfriend — in Hawaii. Then, about a week later, I could return and say something very guy-like, such as, "Hey, at least they all got it over with at once."

But I haven't got the nerve.

I can't even bring myself to leave for a movie with a girlfriend when even one of my children has an upset stomach. Do you know why? Because I'm a mom.

If only guys could understand some of what a mom goes through. While trying to explain the pressure a pregnancy puts on a woman's back, I *almost* talked Bob into a "simple science experiment."

"Let's help you experience this with me," I said as we walked into the pantry and I picked up a fifteen-pound bag of potatoes. "Let's get a bungee cord and strap this around your middle. Then you walk around for a week until the extra weight starts to make your back ache and you gain a realistic view of why I'm a bit edgy at times."

But Bob declined. It seems the Air Force has a regulation against pilots flying government jets with a bag of taters strapped to their belly.

I still don't think my attitude was ever as bad as Bob says it was, but I do remember feeling extreme frustration while trying to exercise when we were expecting Joshua. I had Daniel (age seven) on a bike, Philip (age five) and Bethany (age three) in a double stroller, and Jonathan (age one) in a backpack. Of course, the baby whale was out front. It was tough to push that stroller and balance Jonathan on a tired back with my expanded middle leading the way. It gave new meaning to the verse, "She was great with child."

I used to walk three miles three times a week, right up until the last few weeks of pregnancy. But the thing that bothered me the most was not the physical exertion, it was the way people gave me "the look." I'd walk down the road and people would drop jaws and stare. Oh, sure, some were more subtle than others. Some would just give us a sidelong glance. Others would openly gape.

Bob said that one time the operations officer was driving home for lunch with his windows down and saw me staring at a motorcycle driver who had slowed down for a better look. This "friend" told Bob he overheard me say, "What are *you* lookin' at?"

All moms have good days and bad days. We have memory-making days we cherish, and hair-raising days we can't wait to forget. The important thing to remember is that we need to watch what we say, even on the bad days. But when we do fail, there is more than enough grace to cover us — if we'll just ask God.

. . . .

Set a guard over my mouth O LORD;
keep watch over the door of my lips.

PSALM 141:3

mom's mannequin

Jeanne Zornes

....

My father's salary was very small, so there were economies of every kind. Mother had learned to sew by a Singer Sewing Machine company correspondence course, and she did ingenious things with fabric bought on sale — remnants.

EDITH SCHAEFFER

*Y*ou want to do *what?*" I gasped when Mom presented her plans for my Saturday.

A little later I found myself clad in one of Dad's gauzy, ready-for-rags T-shirts, raising my arms while Mom plastered my upper torso with wide strips of paper dipped in flour-and-water paste.

I knew about papier-mâché for kids' crafts. I'd once covered a balloon to make a miniature earth for a science project. But a papier-mâché project of *me?*

My fate was sealed by mother's frustration in sewing my clothes. I had the figure of a celery stalk and she had to constantly adjust any pattern to fit me — and I wasn't always around at the right time. A commercial dress mannequin was beyond her means, so she decided to make her own. She already had a foam plug for the neck and a broomstick to mount "Jeanne's Double" in an old flagpole stand. All she needed was my discomfort for an hour or so.

"Bake, sun, bake!" I muttered after the grand wrap, sitting on a stool outside while my life wasted away. I was dripping too much to stay inside. Finally Mom deemed me dry enough to cut me free with a careful slit up the back, and my "double" spent another week on newspapers in the garage stiffening up.

Mom meant well. Growing up in the Depression as the oldest of nine born to an immigrant farmer, she knew poverty and improvising. She'd also embraced a thrift ethic that favored sewing over buying clothes. Most of my wardrobe came from bargain remnants Mom stored in a cavernous drawer in the hall linen closet.

"I've been thinking about this dress length," she'd call out to me as I wrestled with geometry homework a room away. I'd dutifully show up at the "sewing drawer" to give my opinion as to whether the fabric seemed compatible with the drawing in the pattern company flyer.

"I thought this was cute," she went on. "Nobody will have a dress like this."

I'd pause, pleased that Mom wanted to make me something, but reluctant in case I'd look too different from my peers.

In a few days, the dress would hang on "Jeanne's Double." I avoided going into the sewing room where the decapitated mummy held my new outfit, waiting the hem-pinning fitting. My shoulders weren't that slumped — or were they? Was I really that fat?

Then came the day I'd first wear it.

"New outfit?" a friend would say at school.

"Yeah, my mom sewed it."

"Sewed it? Wow, my mom can barely mend socks."

Sewing was my mom's love language. We didn't have much money — Dad worked in a paper mill — but she wanted her two daughters to have nice clothes. Maybe she was responding to the scarcities of her own childhood. She never had colorful, crisp taffeta formals, like she sewed for my sister. Or ruffled Sunday dresses of pastel dotted swiss, like she made for me.

A quarter century has passed since my mother died. The homemade papier-mâché dress form is now mush in some landfill. But as I think back on her sewing skills, I realize she offered me a special symbol of God's love. Left to myself, I'd slump around life, dowdy with negative attitudes and destructive actions. But the King of the Universe cares how the world sees me. He has a special garment for me, his princess, made of the most beautiful and costly cloth, purchased at the Cross. It's called the robe of righteousness. Best of all, God doesn't need a mannequin to fit it to me. Because he created me, he knows me inside and out.

Sometimes, when I am sewing, I think back to my teen years and Mom marking hems on my new dresses. This was the sixties, and miniskirts had started to raise hemlines and eyebrows. I wanted to look like the others — and she wanted me to be modest.

"Turn," she'd mumble, pins between her lips and a yardstick next to the hemline.

"Is it just above the knees?" I'd question.

"Just where it should be," she'd say.

I imagine God was smiling.

* *

I delight greatly in the LORD; my soul rejoices in my God.
For he has clothed me with garments of salvation
and arrayed me in a robe of righteousness.

ISAIAH 61:10

bunny tales

Ellie Kay

*A Christian is a person who feels repentance on Sunday for what
he did Saturday and is going to do again on Monday.*

LAURENCE J. PETER

*E*ver since she was old enough to hold a crayon and find an empty wall, our daughter, Bethany, has been in the creative business of writing and drawing. She earned the nickname "Bunny" because when she was two years old, she made us read *ABC Bunny* and *No, No, Bunny* from the Cottontail series a gazillion times.

She enjoyed not only reading but also creating. By the time she was five, she had created some 5,247 works of art. We posted them on our refrigerator, my desk, Bob's work computer, and even the toilet seat cover. I couldn't bear to throw them away, so I shipped them by the boxful to grandparents, aunts, and uncles as our way of keeping in touch with family. But just like another bunny, she kept going, and going, and going. . . . Bethany's creations multiplied as quickly as bunnies do, and I

63

knew if she ever found any of her treasures in the trash, it would traumatize her for life.

What's a mother to do? I started including a drawing in the payment envelope when we mailed the bills — the gas, electric, and phone company all received brightly colored pages from her "Peter Cottontail" coloring book, carefully signed, "Love Bunny."

I was committed to building her self-esteem, so I brought along a few with me in the van when I ran errands. The teller at the bank received a rather cryptic but lovely crayon drawing of a bunny hopping through some tulips. The dry cleaners proudly displayed "Flowers and Puppies" on their window. Even the auto mechanic took down his *Sports Illustrated* cover to put up her "Mama Kitty" drawing and didn't even charge me for repairing our flat tire.

When I got pulled over for speeding one time, I encouraged Bethany to hand one over to the police officer. She was only three at the time and sat proudly in her car seat, her blonde hair gathered on top of her head like Pebbles from *The Flintstones*. She flashed her bright blue eyes and happy teeth as she thrust a coloring of a pink blob through the window.

"What do you think that is?" she asked, convinced that the policeman stopped us to get one of these treasures.

"Uh . . . " he was completely taken off guard as he looked into her bright, eager eyes.

"Uh," he repeated, "it looks like a pink . . . uh, thing?"

"That's right," she squealed. "It's my pink shoe. I ride it. Like my brudders ride der bike! We can go now, Mama, the policey-man got his picture!"

I turned my glance from Bunny's face and looked at the previously stern officer. My eyes saw a reflection of what he found in my daughter's innocent and eager countenance. He caved. Big time. The pressure of a Mama Rabbit and her Bunny was just too much. So, instead of a much-deserved ticket, he gave me a warning.

"Ma'am, you were going forty in a thirty. You need to slow down in the future. And uh," he turned toward Bethany, "thanks for letting me catch up with you so I could get my picture."

Unfortunately, that brush with the law only encouraged me. I began to stick her "cottage industry products" on the rearview mirror in the car, the bathroom mirror, and my compact powder mirror. So whenever I looked into a mirror, I saw a reflection of my little Bunny.

Bethany's outgoing personality suited our military lifestyle. Bob and I were geographically separated from family the second year of our marriage, and we've never lived within 1,000 miles of our extended family since. So the new "friends" Bethany picked up along the way were there to encourage her (okay, they fawned over her) the way her grandparents would have if they had lived nearby.

But our bunny's talents remind me of something else: God looks at us with the same measure of love and compassion that we look at our children. Just as the police officer showed mercy, God loves to extend mercy to us — not because he weakly "caves," but because he can. So the next time you deserve justice and beg for mercy, think about how you can demonstrate this quality in the lives of your kids. And don't forget to throw a few works of kid art into the glove compartment — it might help mercy along the next time you absentmindedly roll a bit faster than the speed limit.

Blessed are the merciful, for they shall receive mercy.

MATTHEW 5:7 NASB

the wedding dress

Pauline Afman

· ·

Once again, mother's very real bank account had provided the necessary provision at a time of need. From those hours spent alone with God each day had come her supreme confidence that he would provide out of his limitless supply.

CATHERINE MARSHALL

he year was 1970. My firstborn, Carol Joy, had married the year before and now daughter number two, Jennie Beth, was engaged — and she needed a wedding dress. My husband and I had decided many years earlier that it was okay to have a credit card, but not to use it unless we knew we would have the money to pay the balance in total when the bill arrived. We discussed the purchase of Jennie's dress and decided that if we were careful, we could spend $100 for the dress. My husband was the pastor of a small church, and we had six children. Finances were tight.

Jennie and I excitedly planned our shopping excursion, and we were almost ready to go out the door, but stopped. We decided to pray about our purchase before we left, asking the Lord to help us find just the right dress at just the right price. The importance of prayer was a lesson I had learned years earlier from my own mother.

Suddenly, there was a knock at the door and in came my dear friend Janet. She attended our church and also participated in the ladies' Bible study I led. It was a joy to see her learn about the Christian life, and she had a personality that always brightened the room. I thought, *I hope she doesn't stay too long; we must get going.* I told her we were about to leave to go shopping for Jennie's wedding dress, hoping she would understand that we didn't have time to chat.

Janet smiled warmly, saying she couldn't stay, but that the Lord had laid it on her heart to give us some money to help pay for Jennie's dress. Then she handed me a check, smiled again, told us to have a good trip, and left.

I heaved a sigh of relief and looked at the check. It was made out for $25. When I told Jennie, we looked at each other and both of us celebrated the same thought: *Now we can get a dress for $125!* We got in the car and sang on our drive to the city.

Arriving downtown at Sperry's Department Store, we made our way to the bridal department and began looking at the dresses. The clerk was busy with a customer so we continued our search, praying the Lord would lead us to just the right dress. Most of the wedding gowns were much too expensive. I checked tag after tag, and my heart sank as I envisioned my daughter's disappointment.

Jennie wandered off to another area in the bridal department and suddenly I heard her cry out, "Oh, Mother! This is the dress I want! I just *love* it! Isn't it *beautiful?*"

There she stood with her face beaming, clutching an exquisite satin gown covered in lace and seed pearls, which she held pressed to her chest.

"How much is it, honey?" I asked cautiously.

"I don't know, Mom," she said, "I couldn't find the tag." A bit of the excitement drained from her voice. "It truly is beautiful, though, isn't it?"

I carefully checked the neckline and sleeves, looking for the price tag, but there didn't seem to be one. Then I checked the other dresses on the rack where she had found her treasure. They didn't have tags either.

"Oh, honey," I said, "it must be very expensive. None of these gowns have price tags on them."

"Couldn't we just ask?" she begged. "Please, Mom, just ask the clerk. This is the dress I really want!"

Just then the clerk arrived to see if she could help us.

"Well, we were wondering how much this dress is," I asked, mentally steeling myself for her response. "We couldn't find the price tag."

Jennie was waiting eagerly for the clerk's answer, and in my heart I prayed that she wouldn't be too disappointed about the price. This was such an exciting day for her, but it seemed that the dresses in this store were simply not in our price bracket.

The clerk hesitated a moment and then said, "Oh, you don't want one of *these* wedding gowns. They've been on display in our window and they all need to be dry-cleaned."

"Oh, but this is the dress I like the best of *all!*" Jennie responded a bit desperately.

Looking at Jennie and then at me, the woman suddenly smiled and shocked us with her next statement. "Of course, if you're willing to have the dress dry-cleaned yourself, you can have it for $25."

Jennie squealed and headed for the fitting room. I felt slightly dazed as I thanked the clerk and told her that if the dress fit, we'd take it.

The dress was a perfect fit. No alterations were needed. God had given me an opportunity to share in a visible answer to prayer with my daughter. We sang his praises all the way home.

Don't worry about anything; instead, pray about everything; tell God your needs and don't forget to thank him for his answers. If you do this you will experience God's peace, which is far more wonderful than the human mind can understand. His peace will keep your thoughts and hearts quiet and at rest as you trust Christ Jesus.

PHILIPPIANS 4:6–7 LB

mom on the run

Ellie Kay

....

*I've learned that you can't have everything and do everything
at the same time.*

OPRAH WINFREY

When my parents retired from the Air Force Reserves, they moved from California back to their roots in Texas. They covered a lot of open territory as they caravaned down the road. One day my Spanish *mamacita* was flying over the open road and down a lonely desert highway in New Mexico in her Mercedes 280SL sports car when she got pulled over by the highway police. The officer stuck his head in the window of her car and asked, "Excuse me, ma'am, do you know how fast you were going?"

My mom emphatically replied, "Jes, I go eightee-five."

The officer was solemn. "Yes, ma'am, that's twenty miles over the speed limit."

The little woman was incensed. "No! It is *not*! I saw sign. It say eightee-five, and I no go more than eightee-five! I no should get no ticket because I go what the sign say."

The policeman's face flushed. "Ma'am, that's *highway* 85. The *speed limit* is still sixty-five miles per hour."

Paquita suddenly became quiet. "Oh." She paused a moment. "It has been many jears since I drive deeze highways. I thought it fast, but maybe, I say to myself, maybe these people in New Mexico, they like to go eightee-five."

She peered up at him. "Are chew going to give me a ticket?"

The officer, whose mood had gone from solemn to trying to stifle his laughter, smiled and answered, "No, ma'am, I'm not. Just slow down to sixty-five. You're the best thing that has happened to me today."

. . . .

It's a good thing my *mamacita* talked to the officer and didn't try to outrun him. If she had, we could have called her a "Mom on the Run." Have you ever felt like a mom on the run? I think most moms, at one time or another, feel they have to run at top speed just to keep up with the kids. Mom's Taxi Service often puts us on the open road a good percentage of our day. It's important for our children to be involved in a variety of activities, but it's equally easy to get overcommitted in the name of "But my child wants to participate in ballet, soccer, and band!" We do all this in the name of "enrichment" and "well-rounded kids." If you multiply those activities times the number of children you have and then throw in mom's and dad's activities, you have the potential for a runaway train — with *you* as the conductor.

With five children at home, we have a "one thing well" rule, and it still puts as much as two hundred miles a day on our car. (That's in a very small town that I call a remote tribal village.) Talk through the pros and cons of each activity with your children and help them decide what they would really like to be involved in. Maybe a child will decide to play soccer one season and start guitar lessons when the soccer season is over. Or when they realize how much time is involved in being on a track team, they may decide to join a weekly scouting program instead. For example, in our family our daughter Bethany plays the violin (with lessons) instead of taking guitar. For sports she's chosen basketball instead of ballet in the fall, and volleyball instead of track during the spring. We discussed the pros and cons of each of these activities, and she made the choices.

When it comes to a mom on the run, we have to do what's best for our families. Our neighbors may have their children involved in a number of activities, and that tends to put pressure on us. We think, "If I'm a good mom, I need to let Sammy play soccer, go to Boy Scouts, and play basketball, too. That's what Nancy does for her son. My little guy deserves the same opportunities." Horsefeathers! No one knows your schedule, your family, and your child the way you do. Even if you sense disapproval in the well-meaning advice of other parents, you and your spouse have to make the hard calls that protect your offspring from becoming a hurried child.

Discuss boundaries with your spouse, set limits, and let the children know what they will be able to do and what they cannot do and why. The benefits are twofold: (1) you won't be a mom on the run, and (2) you'll get fewer speeding tickets. And with all the money you save on traffic fines, you can take your girlfriend out to lunch.

There is a time for everything ... A time to keep and a time to throw away.

ECCLESIASTES 3:1, 6 NLT

facing the fox fur!

Charlotte Adelsperger

. . . .

Most smiles are started by another smile.

14,000 Quips & Quotes

I'll never forget a 1950s family trip through West Virginia when I was about thirteen. My twin sister, Alberta, our brother Wally, and I sat scrunched in the backseat of the car.

"It's so different here, isn't it?" Mother said as we bounced on back roads of poverty-ridden Appalachia. Having left the main highway, our parents took us "exploring."

"Some of these people are struggling just to live," our father said in a caring tone.

Then it happened. As we passed a paintless shack in the woods, Mother thumped Dad's hand. "Stop! See that sign?"

There it was — "FURS FOR SALE." A string of fox furs, faces dangling, hung on a line near the house.

"Want to take a look?" Dad asked.

"Sure, it'll be an adventure," Mother said. Then she turned to us. "You kids stay in the car." I rolled my eyes as our parents sauntered up to the house.

"Hope nobody comes out with a shotgun," Wally mumbled.

A burly man and a frail woman with a friendly smile came out in the yard. They pulled a couple of furs from the line, but we couldn't hear what they said. Then, to our amazement, our parents followed them inside the shack.

Finally, when they came out, Mother had a reddish fox fur draped over her shoulders, its glassy-eyed head greeting us.

Giggling like school children, Mother and Dad climbed into the car. "The woman was so cute," Mother told us. "She'd wrap a fur around me and point me to a little smoky mirror. Then she'd say, 'You look so purr-dee.' Your father insisted we buy this one."

As an idealistic teenager, my face tightened. I thought my parents were being ridiculous! Having watched our pennies on the trip, why would they spend $10 for a silly fox stole? But almost immediately it brought our family a lot of smiles and fun. We kids took turns looking into its face and stroking its coat.

As we drove along Mother described the inside of the couple's house. "They were very poor," she said, her voice dropping. "Maybe we helped a little — and brought some cheer."

Months later I realized our mother had modeled more than a fur; she showed us there's a time to be frivolous — and perhaps an opportunity to help someone else at the same time.

Through the years Mother lived out the joyful side of her Christian faith. She initiated a motto we still remember today: "Let's have family fun!" And she saw to it that we did.

After I married, Mother lived miles away, but we talked often by phone and shared letters. Almost every letter she wrote spoke of her loving prayers for us. I often recall a quote she sent me years ago from an Agnes Sligh Turnbull novel: "Each day is a little life. Fill its hours with gladness if you can; with courage if you can't."

Mother is no longer on this earth, and we miss her deeply. But rich memories — and her laughter — linger on. One Thanksgiving, Mother spontaneously included in her table prayer: "I want always to be remembered to have said that, 'No matter how dark a situation is, God is in charge.'" She wanted us to count on God's faithfulness and to remember joyful family times.

Now I smile when I think back to moments with Mother's fox fur. When a group of girls came to a slumber party, my sister Alberta and I snuck it out of the closet. We slipped it over the shoulders of an innocent pajama-clad friend. She shivered and screamed, then saw its beady eyes and shrieked! We rolled on the floor laughing.

Fortunately, Mother heeded my advice: "Don't wear that thing to church. Any kid sitting behind you will keep petting it!"

* *

May God our Father himself and our Master Jesus clear the road to you! And may the Master pour on the love so it fills your lives and splashes over on everyone around you.

1 Thessalonians 3:11–12 MSG

ernest goes home to school

Ellie Kay

....

It's been said, "Cheer up, things could be worse."
I cheered up and things got worse.

DAVID ROPER

*B*ecause we moved so much in those early years, we homeschooled in order to provide stability and continuity to our children's education. We chose this education option because one of our boys didn't start reading until he was in the fourth grade. Yet, when his language skills finally clicked, he made up three grade levels in six months.

We would dedicate a room to school, and we bought five desks from the turn of the century. During school, the kids called me Mrs. Kay, and I ruled with an iron fist. Homeschooling was never a fearsome task for me because life as a military wife had toughened me up quite a bit. I considered myself a home-front veteran, a road warrior who could get 20,000 pounds of household goods settled in three days or less.

But every Achilles has its heel and mine made its debut when we lived in northern New York.

We were at Fort Drum, which had snow on the ground as many as nine months out of the year. The snow was about four feet deep in the yard, and we were snug and warm in our homeschool classroom. The kids were trying their hand at distracting the teacher, and she was threatening to call the principal (aka Dad) on the phone. This senior homeschool administrator was also the commander of a large Air Support Operations Squadron, and as such he had frequent meetings with his staff.

A child raised his hand. "Can I call Papa . . . um, I mean, the principal? I wanna ask him to take me to the store to get my army man when he comes home."

"No, you can't. He's in a staff meeting and that can wait. Now do your math."

Another child queried, "Can I go to the bathroom?" then for added emphasis started dancing next to his desk. "I *really* got to go!"

It was getting wearisome until one of the kids suddenly stood up and exclaimed, "I just saw a mouse run from behind the bookcase up against the wall!"

I knew it was another stall tactic. "You sit down and stop pretending. It was probably a shadow coming in the window, not a mouse."

Then I felt something scurry over my foot as the kids stood up and we all panicked like the chickens in *Chicken Run* when their lives were threatened.

"AAAARGH!"

"Ooooh Noooo!"

"Help me! *Somebody* help me!"

"AAAAHHH!"

Ten-year-old Daniel had the presence of mind to call and get Bob out of a staff meeting. The rest of us were standing on desks and chairs, watching the trapped mouse scramble amidst human screams trying to find a way of escape. I was standing on top of "Mrs. Kay's" desk with my skin crawling when Daniel handed me the phone and calmly said, "It's Papa."

"Beloved, is everything all right?" he asked with concern in his voice as he heard screams of hysteria in the background.

"Does it sound like everything's all right? There's a mouse in the house, and you must come home right now! I will do two-thousand-mile moves, I'll have a baby alone, I'll even play single mom to these kids while you're in harm's way. I'll do a lot of things. But I will not ever, under any circumstances, do rodents!"

I once saw a scary movie as a child that featured rats tormenting a prisoner, and I've been deathly afraid of them ever since. Our school administrator (Dad) told his staff there was an "emergency at home," and he was home within five minutes. The mouse had chased everyone, except Daniel, into the kitchen, and I was standing on top of the kitchen counter, sobbing and holding my children next to me.

Bob quickly trapped the mouse and told the teacher to dismiss class for the rest of the day and go to McDonald's. Many days later, when I had recovered my wits, Bob told me what I really looked like in my rare moment of complete panic. He said that my teeth were exposed, my mouth was wide open, and my eyes were bugged out. He couldn't help but think that I looked just like Jim Varney in those *Ernest* movies. In other words I looked like a complete fool.

I was *not* amused.

Ya know what I mean, Vern?

This mom and former teacher was really glad she had someone to help her on days when life (and a mouse) chased her into a dither. When Bob is gone, God sends other angels of mercy at just the right time. And yet there are moments when there's no husband within calling distance, I get my friends' answering machines, and my neighbors are out running errands. Then I must handle the circumstance all "alone."

But I also know that is exactly where God wants me at times. Women tend to be so relational that we run to a spouse, a mom, a mentor, a friend, or a pastor, and we forget to run to God *first* with our crisis du jour. So whether you have a mouse in your house or a fool in your school, know that God is there with you and he will send his helpers at just the right moment.

. . . .

Two people can accomplish more than twice as much as one;
they get a better return for their labor. If one person falls, the
other can reach out and help. But people who are alone when
they fall are in real trouble.

ECCLESIASTES 4:9–10 NLT

this isn't the life i signed up for!

Jill Lynnele Gregory

. . . .

*May I be patient! It is so difficult to make real what one believes,
and to make these trials, as they are intended, real blessings.*

John Henry Newman

My life had sunk to a new low. My son, who attracts dirt like a magnet, needed a good soak in the bathtub before I could scrub him down, put him in his pj's, and tuck him in for the night.

There is no "polite" way to explain what happened next. I stooped down next to the tub and discovered my not-so-charming child had pooped in his bath water. As I tried to get "it" out of the tub, the elusive remains of my son's bowel movement kept getting away from me. With one hand I tried to keep my toddler away from the problem area, and with toilet paper in the other hand I dived in like a bomber pilot in search of my target. After cleaning up this stinky mess, I had to bathe my son all over again.

In the middle of my exasperation I called my mother. "Mom, I just spent the last ten minutes bobbing for poop. I can't believe I went to college for *this*!"

I wish I could say that was the last major surprise in my career as a mother. My husband and I had four children in three and half years, including twin daughters. Our life was busy, but we were surviving because *I had a system!* My carefully prepared daily agenda included a plan to change the diapers, feed the children, and schedule nap times. When my system worked, I felt in control. Then came a new challenge, and I knew this wasn't the job I had signed up for.

One of my twin daughters seemed to be a dreamer. She would go off by herself and stare intently at books or at videocassette covers. We first thought she was an introspective, reflective soul, and then one day I looked at my husband and said, "Does Sarah really say *anything*?" We knew she could say her name or Mama or Dada, but she hadn't called us by those names for quite a while. Sarah seemed to ignore us, but she turned around when I dropped a book behind her.

When I consulted with Sarah's pediatrician, I was not prepared for his preliminary diagnosis. "Jill, I think it's autism." My mind raced. *What? How can this be? Autism? Isn't that what Dustin Hoffman's character had in the movie* Rain Man? *Sarah isn't like that character!*

I was desperate for a different answer. *Maybe it's her hearing,* I thought. *Maybe she needs ear tubes.* But Sarah's hearing tests came back normal. My husband and I went to the school system for an evaluation and, although they agreed with our pediatrician, according to state laws they could not diagnose her as autistic until age three.

Sarah's school evaluation was given to us on the same day as our oldest child's fifth birthday. To hear from an additional source that our beautiful daughter might be autistic was a hard blow. Our nagging suspicions were being confirmed. The next day was the birthday party, and I held back the tears for the next twenty-four hours until the last child left the celebration. Then I mourned.

I also had a little discussion with God. Through tears I cried, *God, this was not part of my plan! My twin girls were going to be best friends! They were going to have tea parties, paint nail polish on each other's toes, and do fun girl things together. The twins were going to stay up late, share secrets, and giggle. How could you allow this to happen?*

I experienced a prolonged grieving process. I didn't want to admit the truth of my daughter's diagnosis. After many months, my anger and pain turned to grieving for Sarah. In *Kisses of Sunshine for Sisters* I explain the remarkable support of my sisters during this unexpected challenge in our lives. My sister Leanne volunteered to care for my children when I took Sarah to specialists and attended conferences that have helped me understand my daughter's challenges. My sister Laura stepped down from a managerial position in a large company, choosing to work part time, so she could assist me with Sarah's therapy. Moving from *my* plan for my family to God's plan for my family has been a long, hard process. But I'm learning that I can find joy "even in *this*."

Sarah's official medical evaluation now shows she has moderate autism, and her progress has been remarkable. She is speaking words and responding appropriately to questions. I still occasionally revert to "fixing things," but I'm learning this journey is a process and God loves Sarah even more than I do.

. . . .

One day my mind went back to the day I called my Mom because I had to be a "pooper-scooper mother," which doesn't require a college degree, just "on-the-job-training." I can honestly smile now, realizing that my life has taken a more difficult turn than I expected, but I am learning firsthand that I have a God of refuge who is my Comforter and my Teacher. He has given me the important job of loving a special-needs child and of sharing my story with other mothers who have had unexpected "job descriptions" in their own roles as parents.

God has placed a smile on my face that can only come from him. This is not the life I signed up for, but it's the assignment God has for me today.

. . . .

All praise to the God and Father of our Lord Jesus Christ. He is the source of every mercy and the God who comforts us. He comforts us in all our troubles so that we can comfort others. When others are troubled, we will be able to give them the same comfort God has given us.

2 CORINTHIANS 1:3–4 NLT

growing into his feet

Ellie Kay

....

*Parents spend two years teaching children to walk and talk and
eighteen years trying to get them to sit down and be quiet.*

TED ENGSTROM

*D*aniel was fifteen months old and still not walking so we took him to the pediatrician, who said
he needed special shoes. These $150 shoes
were white and chunky, and they worked — he was walking and
running with the other toddlers within weeks. His shoes were so
heavy and solid that when Bob hoisted Daniel to ride on his
shoulders one time, Daniel accidentally kicked Bob in the forehead, causing a gash so deep I thought we were going to have
to get Bob some stitches.

Today his shoes are still unusual. Just ask his basketball
coach. Daniel, as the new kid in the high school, shyly went by
the coach's office to see if he could sign up for basketball. The
coach was sitting behind his desk with his assistant by his side

when Daniel's six-foot-four-inch frame blocked the light coming in from the doorway.

The coach's mouth dropped open as the assistant asked, "What size shoe do you wear?" (I guess you can tell how tall a kid will be by the size of his feet in the early high school years.)

"A size fifteen, sir," Daniel replied.

The assistant leaned forward in his chair. "A size *fifteen* shoe?"

The head coach echoed him. "A size *fifteen* shoe?"

At that moment, the football coach was walking past the office and Daniel heard a voice booming from the hallway, "Did you say a size *fifteen* shoe?"

Our "little" boy celebrated his fifteenth birthday this year with four other big-footed friends. We have a shoe rack in the garage where the kids pile their sneakers before they enter the house. I returned home from the pizza shop to find that Daniel's friends had already arrived. There on the rack were two pairs of size twelve tennis shoes, a size thirteen, a size fifteen, and an astonishing size sixteen. The coaches would have been in heaven.

The big-footed boys were inside, playing PlayStation 2 like a bunch of overgrown puppy dogs who were destined to accommodate their feet. They were polite, awkward teenagers, content to be eating pizza and chowing down on homemade chocolate cake with butter-cream frosting. As I watched Daniel open his presents, bashfully thanking each person for their gift, I thought back to his first pair of walking shoes. Where had my little guy gone?

But another, more sobering thought struck me as I watched the son of whom I am so proud. When Daniel was little, I began to have babies one right after the other. We moved many times in just a few years. Daniel didn't get much of my time because he was the oldest of so many in our challenging military lifestyle. As I watched, my heart began to ache with questions:

"My son, did I hug you enough? Did I take the time to kiss you and ruffle your hair before you became too big for such things? I was so busy and you grew up so fast! Did I love and kiss on you enough, my son?"

. . . .

Bob insists that I did cuddle and snuggle Daniel enough when he was a baby, but I still wonder. So now, even though Daniel can't sit in my lap without squashing me, I make a point to hug him often and kiss him good-night — he's not too big for that. One day soon, he'll leave the house, and I don't want any regrets. Our teens — boys and girls — need hugs and kisses on the cheek and even a playful slug on the arm. So don't forget to continue the physical contact with your older kids, especially hugs. For me, it gives me great comfort as my babies grow into their feet.

. . . .

Encourage the young women to love their husbands,
to love their children.

Titus 2:4 NASB

beaus and bathtubs

Bonnie Afman Emmorey

. . . .

A lasting gift to a child is the gift of
a parent's listening ear — and heart.

14,000 QUIPS AND QUOTES

Replaying memories of high school and dating puts many people into a sweat. While I have vivid recollections of awkwardness and embarrassment, one sweet memory centers on my mother. She was always in the bathtub when I would get in from a date. Whatever time I arrived home, the first place I headed was to the bathroom.

There I would find Mother — up to her neck in bubbles. I would perch myself on the throne and share all the details of my evening. Mother would listen, smile, and give wise counsel. Those evenings were sweet. I remember laughter erupting at unexpected moments, followed by her deep empathy for my silly mistakes. In that atmosphere, my mother became my closest confidant. She loved me and made me know that my secrets were safe. I knew that she was interested in everything about me, and she made even the smallest details worthy of good listening skills. It was during that time my mother became one of my best friends.

. . . .

Many years later I was a married woman with two sons entering the dating years. I thought long and hard about what I had experienced. Obviously I couldn't use the bathroom as my center for conversations with my boys following their dates, but I longed to create that same atmosphere of warmth, love, and safety that my mother provided for me.

I came up with a plan. *Hot chocolate!* I would have the hot water ready, with mugs on the table, just waiting for my sons when they would arrive home from a date. It's true that I never quite reached the same level of in-depth sharing with them that Mother and I experienced, but our "Hot Chocolate Talks" did launch a wonderfully open communication that has lasted well into their young adult years.

. . . .

Recently, the bathtub played another important role in my "Mother Memories." Mom was having some serious health issues, and it was a joy to have her stay in our home for over six weeks. We spent many hours playing games and talking to each other. We took daily walks downtown, went window-shopping, and laughed a lot.

One day I said, "Mother, why don't you take a long, hot bath?" Since we now live in an old Victorian home, our bathtub is from a different era — the old soaker variety. With Mom's severe back problems, it is very difficult for her to get up from a down position. As a result, she hasn't been able to take baths for many years. After convincing her that I could assist in getting her out of the tub, she consented.

Oh, what fun we had that day! Mother had taught me how to crochet a couple of years earlier, and I was working on an afghan for one of my sisters. So while Mother soaked in the tub, I pulled a comfy rocking chair into the bathroom and crocheted as we talked and laughed, savoring the moments. We remembered those post-date bathtub sessions from the past. We talked about my sons and their girlfriends. We shared our personal concerns.

After two sweet hours of soaking, Mother's skin resembled that of a prune, but we both knew we had made a lasting memory. Our communication was freer and our mother-daughter bond was even stronger. Long will I relive that day in my "precious memories file" and enjoy again the warmth, love, and safety of our bathtub talks.

* * *

But whoever listens to me will live in safety and be at ease, without fear of harm.

PROVERBS 1:33

nick news at night

Ellie Kay

....

Due to unforeseen circumstances, no clairvoyant meeting will be held tonight until further notice.

UNION-SUN AND JOURNAL, QUOTED IN QUOTE UNQUOTE

*N*ational television? Who, me?" thirteen-year-old Philip asked as I told him the news that he had been chosen to represent the Christian point of view for a news special on Nickelodeon because of some contacts I had with a production assistant.

"What do they want me to discuss?" He sat down on the couch in my home office, clearly excited about the prospect of being on television.

"Homosexuality."

Philip's eyes bugged out. "I'm supposed to talk about that on national television?"

Our son was smack in the middle of the transition from childhood to adulthood. At six-foot-one he had the body of a man but still wanted the reliable comforts of childhood. This was a decision he would have to make on his own. He would have to grapple with the pros and cons of this trip to New York. He knew we would support him whatever he decided. We never could have foreseen this kind of challenge for him at this age.

I remembered when he was a five-year-old playing in the sandbox with a friend. This little friend didn't attend church regularly, and Philip had already memorized many Bible verses. He understood them. We knew, even when he was young, that God had a very special plan for this boy — if our son could bring into balance the zeal of a prophet that burned within him.

After Philip and his friend played for a while, I heard shouting and went outside to investigate. Apparently they were talking about Easter, and the other boy said, "Easter isn't about Jesus rising from the dead! It's about egg hunts and the Easter bunny!"

The shouting I heard was Philip. "What do you mean it's about bunnies and not Jesus? You'd better take that back!" He grabbed the other boy and pulled him to his feet and then continued his diatribe, "You'd better take that back, or you're going to *hell*!"

Yep, it took some more training to teach our little evangelist that this method of sharing the good news wasn't good to the person receiving it.

But now, with the offer to be on national television, this man-child had an opportunity to have a much broader audience, and he had learned the fact that God is a God of justice *and* mercy.

Nickelodeon would fly each student panelist, along with both parents, to New York. I had a business commitment in Colorado Springs, so Bob would be the one to escort Philip should he decide to go. We helped him research information from biblical, social, and medical perspectives.

In the end, after much prayer and consideration, Philip said, "I believe this is something God wants me to do. Oftentimes, Christians are misrepresented in the media, and I want to show people who are on the opposite side of this issue that God loves them."

Bob and Philip flew to New York City and taped the show with the host, Linda Ellerbee, at the CBS studios. The panel of guests who were to join the student panel was all gay — including a principal, a firefighter hero of 9-11, and Rosie O'Donnell.

Philip was articulate, at ease, and even well-spoken. He made jokes off camera to help the other kids on the set be more at ease.

On the air he said, "I didn't come here to judge anybody but to reach out to them and show them God's love. Some people think that Christians like to judge everybody and think they are perfect. Well, no one is perfect."

He made friends with the daughter of a lesbian couple and writes to her regularly. Rosie O'Donnell was a kind and gracious woman who took the time to chat with the kids and answer their questions about the movies she'd made.

I've been to New York often. Our oldest daughter, Missy, graduated from Columbia University there. I've seen the street preachers that scream:

"You are going to hell!"

"Repent you sinners!"

"Judgment is coming and you will die!"

I guess they were never taught about God's mercy when they were playing in sandboxes with their friends. Where is the genuine love of Christ? Where is the compassion? Can't you love the person and still strongly disagree with what they do? Philip is one of those kids who believes that you can sooner change the world by shining a light in the darkness than you can by cursing at the night.

When the final show was edited and aired, the three Christian kids on the set had their full voice heard. They did not compromise their biblical theology, and they still managed to show kindness. The overall tone of the program was very much pro-homosexual, but we have no regrets about allowing our son to take his own stand to have his voice heard in his generation. Time and eternity will tell what kind of impact his words and actions had.

There may be a time when you will have to allow your teen to take a stand — whether it's praying at the school flagpole, fighting an anti-religious school policy, or even speaking on national television. By allowing your children to grapple with the issues, you will be equipping them to be a light to not only their own generation but for generations that follow.

. . . .

I will send my messenger ahead of you, who will prepare your way — a voice of one calling in the desert, "Prepare the way for the Lord, make straight paths for him."

MARK 1:2 – 3

heart strings

Sandi Banks

. . . .

There is no more influential or powerful role
on earth than a mother's.

CHARLES STANLEY

*M*mmmmm ... the lilting strains of the much-loved hymn "In the Garden" linger in midair, as I lift my fingers gently from the strings of Mom's grand old concert harp. I sit here and breathe a sigh. How I miss her. Memories flood my mind as the familiar lyrics soothe my soul.

I come to the garden alone, while the dew is still on the
  roses,
And the voice I hear falling on my ear, the Son of God
  discloses ...

My mind has pressed "rewind" to a day long gone: August 20, 1956. We had cleaned house, decorated the table with freshly picked roses from our garden, and begun greeting guests. My tenth birthday slumber party, a long-awaited event, had come at last.

All seven little girls promptly gathered like magnets around Mom's harp, awestruck. "I never heard a real harp before." "Play for us, pleeeease?"

So at their insistence, Mom gave a mini-concert for my young friends in the living room of our tiny duplex.

"Beauuuutiful!" "Play another song!" "Wow!"

My friends were animated. My heart was overjoyed.

"Thank you, Mommy," I whispered afterward, as she put the pedals up and smiled. "My very first slumber party -- this is going to be so much fun!"

It was the first time I'd been able to have anyone over since Daddy had left our family and Mom had moved her three daughters to Denver.

"We're so glad you're here!" Mom welcomed my little friends in her typically warm and gracious way. "After dinner, we'll play some games, and open presents and — "

"Hey, where's your Daddy?" My new best friend Sheila interrupted my mom and was facing me squarely.

"Oh . . . umm, he's working," I lied.

"Where's he sleep?"

"In there." I pointed to my mom's closed bedroom door.

Sheila burst into the room, trailed by the others. A single bed. Flowers and lace.

"This is your mommy's room. Where's your *daddy* sleep?"

I felt my face burn red hot. A lump formed in my throat.

"Well, see, he works really hard and comes home really late and he loves us all *so* much that he doesn't want to wake us up so he ... umm ... sleeps downstairs."

No sooner had the words stumbled across my tongue and tumbled out my lips than The Sherlock Seven were descending the basement stairs, relentless in their pursuit.

A ringer washer, a pile of old newspapers, and probably a spider or two greeted them there. The truth became painfully clear to my inquisitive friends. I'd been had.

Incensed, Sheila strutted toward me, knuckles firmly on her hips, eyes ablaze.

"You don't even *have* a daddy, do you!"

Her words pierced my heart. I burst into tears, raced upstairs, locked myself in my room, and made my mom send all the girls and their gifts back home. I sobbed into the night.

> And He walks with me and He talks with me,
> and He tells me I am His own ...

Slowly I lower the harp to the floor. It's been nearly fifty years since that fateful day. Yet the sound of Mom's gentle voice trying to comfort me through that bedroom door remains a poignant memory.

How I wish she were still alive. I want to curl up with her on the couch like we used to do, safe and cozy in our jammies and slippies. I have so many things to ask — questions that come to a daughter only after she's grown and tasted the stark realities of life herself.

What was it like to be a single parent all those years, Mom?

Were you lonely? Did you have anyone you could confide in when it hurt?

Did the responsibilities weigh heavily on your heart?

Did you ever wonder if you would make it in those early years?

And then I would say, woman to woman, wounded heart to wounded heart, "Oh, Mom, I never considered how *you* must have felt that night; I only knew *my* pain. Now I understand. And I love you all the more."

"Where is your daddy?"

We who have struggled with this question can take heart. No matter what our circumstances are, we who put our trust in him need never ask where our father is because our God lovingly assures us — we have a Father in heaven who will always love us, never leave us, and *forever* will call us his beloved daughters.

And the joys we share as we tarry there
None other has ever known.

. . . .

God has said, "Never will I leave you; never will I forsake you."

HEBREWS 13:5

presidential appointment

Ellie Kay

....

President George Bush died and went to heaven. When he entered, he was met by Saint Peter, who asked him if he had any requests. "Yes, I've studied the leadership of Moses and would like to talk to him." When Saint Peter found Moses and told him of President Bush's request, Moses replied, "No way. Last time I talked to a bush, I got forty years."

CHARLES SWINDOLL

We are a family of patriots. My grandfather was a tail gunner who died in service to his country in World War II. My Uncle Dick survived the Bataan death march only to die of pneumonia two weeks later. My dad was in the Navy when he met my mom in Spain, and he retired as an Air Force reservist a couple of years ago. My husband, Bob, has been in the Air Force for over twenty-three years and his blood runs true blue. In short, serving God and country is very important to us. So much so that all four of our sons want to go into the military. We will see how that plays out.

Daniel, Philip, and Jonathan want to attend the United States Air Force Academy, and Joshua wants to become "a snake eater." In layman's terms he wants to go to West Point and then into special operations. Daniel and Jonathan want to fly jets, and Philip wants to become a security forces officer (a cop).

Recently, we learned that George W. Bush was coming to a city within forty-five minutes of where we live. When Bob and I heard that we could get tickets to hear him speak, we were very excited. Due to the nature of the speech and the event, we decided to take Daniel along. The only problem was that Daniel had to get off work at the Dairy Queen. He had been saving toward buying Bob's truck and had been working all summer to get about halfway toward his goal.

I remember the first day Daniel went to work in his DQ hat and his navy blue polo shirt with DQ on the sleeve. He was so proud and I was proud of him. I took his photo at home and hugged him, tweaked his cheek, and said, "Oh, my little boy is growing up."

He tolerated my motherly doting but drew the line at letting me go into the store to take a photo of him clocking in for the first time. I don't understand what his problem was — I promised to be as discreet as a mother following her son with a digital, still, and video camera could be.

On the day before the presidential speech, Daniel tried to get someone else to work for him, but it was a short-handed weekend at DQ. Despite his best efforts, he was unsuccessful.

When Daniel made a final plea to the owner, explaining that this may be the only chance in his life to hear the president speak live, his boss replied, "Well, I expect to see you tomorrow at eleven or I will assume your absence is also your resignation."

Daniel was torn. Slinging hash at a fast-food joint wasn't exactly the same thing as being a Wall Street broker, but it was a job that a fifteen-year-old could hold in a small town. He was active in Junior ROTC and had a great deal of respect for the president. He knew that one day he could even receive (as the son of retired military) a presidential appointment to the Air Force Academy. He really wanted to hear the prez.

But it would cost him his job. We let him decide. After going back and forth, Daniel came to us and said, "You know, if I leave them hanging at Dairy Queen, then it makes my witness as a Christian look pretty lousy. I really want to hear the president, but I've made a commitment to work, and I've got to fulfill it."

Sometimes our kids are faced with difficult decisions that could possibly set a standard they will follow for the rest of their lives. They need to make character an important factor in their decision-making process, and we can guide them toward that end. Our job as parents is to give them enough freedom to fail, but not enough to inflict a serious hit to their integrity. Maybe one day Daniel will meet the president. Maybe he won't.

As rewarding an experience as a presidential speech is, maintaining and keeping your personal integrity is much more valuable. That's a lesson Daniel had to learn for himself.

. . . .

A good name is to be more desired than great wealth.

PROVERBS 22:1 NASB

keeping the groom —
dumping the dress

Allison L. Shaw

. . . .

This above all — to thine own self be true.

Polonius in Hamlet

*M*y best friend and I began planning our weddings in the fourth grade. In flights of romantic fancy, we poured through bridal magazines, clipping out our favorite dresses and pasting them into scrapbooks. You would think that with all that practice, when the day arrived and my Prince Charming popped the question, I would have been more prepared to buy a wedding dress. But in fact, the opposite was true. I panicked.

While visiting my fiancé in California, I pulled out my handy wedding planner and realized that only five months remained until the big day. According to the planner I needed at least three months to shop for a dress, another month to narrow down my choices, four months for the dress to be made, and yet another month for alterations. I was way behind schedule. I jumped in the car and headed for the nearest Bridal Warehouse. Within minutes I was head over heels in a world of tulle and tiaras, swept up in my little-girl fantasies of what a dream wedding dress should be.

I bought a dress, headed home, and put the whole incident out of my mind until the dress arrived a few weeks before the wedding. As I opened the box, a gust of tulle exhaled onto the bed and it just kept on coming. Imagine a magician pulling a trick scarf from a hat, and you can imagine how much tulle was jammed into that box. I slipped the dress over my shoulders, zipped it up, and turned to face the mirror.

I am almost six feet tall and the dress swallowed me whole. I have an hourglass figure, and this dress was designed for a one-hundred-pound, ramrod-straight supermodel. The off-the-shoulder neckline doubled the width of my torso. The bodice's V-shaped drop waist made the clouds of tulle jutting out from my hips look even more ridiculous. I fought back the tears, determined to be brave as I went to show my mom.

"What do you think?" I asked her with a twirl trying to convince myself that if I could fool her, I could fool myself into liking the dress. She hesitated for a moment and said, "You look beautiful." It wasn't a lie. I will always be beautiful to my mom (a lesson I learned when I chopped off all of my hair just days before my senior yearbook pictures). But she wasn't particularly convincing.

As I prepared for bed, I could hold back the tears no longer. I *hated* the dress. I slipped out of my room and found my mom dozing on the couch.

"Mom," I whispered, "I think I've made a mistake."

She bolted upright, her mind racing through a list of possibilities. The wedding was just weeks away — what could be wrong that would render me so stricken?

"What is it?" she asked, wide-eyed with concern. "Do you think you've picked the wrong guy?"

"No, Mom, I *know* I have the right guy," I sobbed, "but I have the *wrong* dress. I feel like the song 'Here comes the bride, big fat and wide.' It's too poufy and froufy. It's just not me."

"Oh Angel, we can fix that," she said, breathing a sigh of relief.

"But it's already paid for and it was expensive and I know how much this wedding is costing you," I cried. "I don't know how to tell Dad."

"You leave that up to me," she said. "No daughter of mine is going to walk down the aisle feeling ugly."

The next morning we bought another wedding dress off the rack. It was simple. It was classic. It was me. My brothers posted signs on local college campuses that said, "Keeping the Groom — Dumping the Dress." We sold the cloud of tulle to another starry-eyed bride, and I walked down the aisle in the dress of my older and wiser dreams.

My mom has taught me a number of love lessons over the years, but reminding me that I am most beautiful when I am being myself is one that continues to remind me of the depths of her unconditional love. I bet she learned that from her heavenly Father.

* * *

I have loved you with an everlasting love; I have drawn you with loving-kindness.

JEREMIAH 31:3

girls under glass

Ellie Kay

....

Jonah swallowed by a fish? I'd believe it if Scripture said Jonah swallowed the fish! It's not difficult to believe if you believe in a God of miracles.

BILLY GRAHAM

We were all together for Bob's milestone flight in the Stealth F-117 fighter. It was a dream come true to have every one of our seven children present for such a significant moment in Bob's career, because not all of the children were raised under the same roof. When we entered the squadron, the kids began to file by the operations desk, where a half dozen pilots stood around getting ready for their flights. One of them dubbed Bob "The Great Procreator." Bob said he felt like Papa from *Fiddler on the Roof* when he was introducing all his daughters to the new tutor. "Now this one is mine. And that one's mine. And that one's mine. And that one's mine ... but that one," pointing to Joshua who stood in his Army camouflage suit, sticking his gum on his nose, "that one is definitely not mine!"

They quickly ushered us into a truck to transport everyone to the flight line. As the official escorts, maintenance personnel, and crew chief went through their pre-flight activities, we watched with pride inside the hangar. Bob climbed into the cockpit, strapped on his jet, and finished his checklist, then he began to pull out of the hangar. We were in awe. All cameras were shut down due to the still top-secret nature of the Stealth. It could not be photographed while moving. Bob passed his operations officer and crew chief, whom he saluted. Then he rolled by his seven kids, several of whom had tears in their eyes, and waved. Finally, he passed me and moved his hand from his heart and flung it in my direction — the signal for "my heart goes out to you." This was a day I had only imagined several years ago but didn't truly believe would happen.

When I was in my early twenties, I used to wonder how adoptive parents could love their children as much as biological parents could. Then I married a man who had two daughters, Missy and Mandy, who were six and eight at the time. They aren't babies of my womb, but they are daughters of my love.

During those early years God gave me an incredible capacity to love, and I honestly felt that I loved them as much as I do my biological children — albeit in a different way. I didn't bond with them at birth, but I hoped to bond with them in my new life with their father.

That's why it was so difficult to "lose" them due to geographical moves and other, more complicated reasons that most blended families understand. We spent way too many years longing to see them, sending cards and gifts that would never reach them, and making phone calls that would not be returned. No wonder God hates divorce. There's nothing pretty about it.

Bob and I had more children, but Missy and Mandy's empty places at our table echoed the empty place in our hearts that only they could fill. I remember crying out to God with an unanswerable one-word prayer:

"Why?"

Why would God put an incredible love in my heart for these girls — only to have them ripped away from the womb of my soul? How would it be better for them to stay where they were rather than be with us? Why didn't God just take away the pain of their absence?

"Why?"

In the midst of those ten long years without our girls, I was looking through a catalog one day and came across an ad for glass doll cases. There were two cases pictured. One contained a china doll that looked like a little girl and the other featured a beautiful bride. At that moment, God spoke to my heart:

See the girls. They are under the covering of my protection. The dust and dirt of these years may get on the cases around them, but it will not touch the girls. Your prayers are also their covering. I will restore them to you one day and they will still be as precious as these collectable china dolls are to those who love them.

I clipped out and dated the picture of the dolls in the catalog and put it on our refrigerator as a reminder of God's word of promise. We prayed regularly for the girls. We kept their photos out and talked about Missy and Mandy to the other children who didn't see them often. I made handcrafted Christmas ornaments for them each year thinking, "One day I want them to know how much they were a part of our lives even though they were not here."

A decade later, when Missy was in college, she called and wanted to see us. The reunion was tenuous at first, and then rapidly the walls came down as we reached into that "glass case" and found the "china doll" to be whole and beautiful. Two years later, Mandy did the same in a different way. It was a desire fulfilled.

Part of being a parent may mean waiting on a child to return to your heart. It may mean there are years of prayer with very little interaction. It oftentimes means turning over the dreams and desires for our children into the hands of a loving God. He is more than capable of bringing his word to pass in due season.

* * *

Hope deferred makes the heart sick,
but a longing fulfilled is a tree of life.

PROVERBS 13:12

perfect timing

Jolanta Hoffmann

Time is too slow for those who wait, too swift for those who fear,
too long for those who grieve, too short for those who rejoice.
But for those who love, time is not.

HENRY VAN DYKE

*S*o, where are you?' my husband called. I was buried in a closet full of children's choir paraphernalia. Ten days before we had relocated to a new pastorate in a small rural town. I had gotten our home settled and was now working on my favorite area of the church, the children's choir closet.

As a box of wrist bells came crashing to the floor, he found me. "Here you are. Linda from the teen-pregnancy center just called. An adoption attorney just called her looking for a couple who would like to adopt two toddlers. The attorney wants us to meet with the birth mother today. What do you think?"

What did I think? I was thrilled! After seven years of prayers, infertility testing, hopes, disappointments, waiting lists, and being "on hold" regarding God's perfect timing to complete our family, I was ready . . . or was I?

We got more information about the situation from the attorney. If we could get the necessary background checks done that day, we could take the children home with us that night. Humanly speaking, there was no way for that to happen. Before we departed for the meeting, we left signatures and forms with my husband's secretary. She assured us, "I'll do everything within my power to get this job done. This is a small town, y'all, and I know everyone!"

We picked up our daughter from school. She was very excited, as she had been asking God to bring her a brother or sister for seven years. We were going to meet in a public place where the children could play together and feel comfortable.

The next moment is forever fixed in my mind. The children were beautiful! We could tell by their bright eyes that they were intelligent and healthy, but we also realized they had been through things most toddlers shouldn't have to experience. Their birth mother, Jennifer, was a nice-looking person who was easy to talk with but nervous about the future of her children. She relayed the details that brought her little family to this point — a plan of adoption.

After several hours, the attorney informed us that my husband's secretary had gotten all of the background checks completed. The children, for whom we had prayed, were going home with us *that night*.

With the legalities completed, Jennifer, the children's biological mother, began her tearful farewell. She told the oldest toddler, "Remember how I told you I am going away for a long time and you are going to get a new mommy and daddy?"

My new daughter nodded in response.

"Well, this lady is going to be your new mommy, and that man over there is going to be your new daddy."

"My daddy?" Her interest was piqued, as "Daddy" had not been in her vocabulary.

Jennifer continued, "You be a good girl and take care of your brother. You'll be able to go to school when you are a little older. I love you." She hugged and kissed both of the children good-bye and then they ran back to play, unable to understand the magnitude of what had just transpired.

It was then the birth mom and the adoptive mom fell into each other's arms. We clung to each other with our tears intermingled, bonding in this heart-wrenching moment. She pleaded with me, "Please take good care of my babies!"

Through my tears I answered, "I will take *very* good care of your babies, and I will always tell them how much you love them."

Heading for home, we were astonished that God had increased our family by two in a matter of hours. That night I slept fitfully. *Had we really made the right decision? Were we really ready for two toddlers at once? Was this really an act of God?* Every time I awakened I felt nauseated. Many worries flooded my mind, but it was a song of assurance by Babbie Mason that calmed my fears. Her lyrics reminded me to "Pray On" and that spiritual battles are always won as we stay on our knees and lift our petitions to God.

. . . .

Several years have passed since this story began, and we are still praying for wisdom as we raise our vibrant, lively children in the ways of the Lord. We are grateful God put us in the right place at the right time, giving us the opportunity to nurture two little lambs who needed safe pasture. God's timing is always perfect.

. . . .

The human mind may devise many plans, but it is the purpose of the LORD that will be established.

PROVERBS 19:21 NRSV

things a dad can't do

Ellie Kay

· ·

No one is poor who had a godly mother.

ABRAHAM LINCOLN

*H*ow are you and the kids doing, honey?" asked the mom on the phone to the dad at home.

"Uh, I'm just watching the game on TV, hon. It's tied at the bottom of the tenth," he replied as he turned up the volume.

"But where are the kids? You know our seven- and five-year-old boys?" She began to get alarmed, knowing her husband could either know the score of the ball game or where the kids were, but he couldn't know both.

"Oh, don't worry, the last I saw them they were out in the south pasture playing by the fishing hole."

That worried mama was home from her luncheon in a flash and found her sons swimming in a slimy green pond, covered from head to toe in tar-like mud.

How come dads can't do things like moms? For example:

- He can't cook dinner, answer math problems, and know that a kid is upstairs getting into a secret chocolate stash — all at the same time.
- He can't cook dinner and wash dishes — it's one or the other.
- He can't pass up a Home Depot, but he can pass over the pile of dirty laundry lying in the hall.
- He can't buy a new vacuum cleaner without calling it a "gift."
- He can't remember to fix the garbage disposal, but remembers who was on third in the final inning of the seventh game of the 1997 World Series when that famous hitter-guy knocked one out of the ballpark.
- He can't understand a simple chick flick, but we expect him to read our minds.
- He never has one of those dreams where he has to go to the bathroom and then wonders, in his dream, if he is going to the bathroom.
- He can't eat a salad lunch and drive at the same time.
- He can't paint his fingernails in the car.
- He can't understand that when you say you don't want to talk what you really mean is that he'd better ask you, "What's wrong?"
- He can't understand that the only right answer to "How do I look in this dress?" is a quick and clear "Great, honey. You look *great*!"
- He can't listen to a problem without trying to fix it.

I think it's safe to say that moms bring something to a child's life that a dad just can't; hard as he tries, he is not and will not ever be a mom. That's why God likes the idea of a mom and a dad in every family. But what if you're a mom and dad isn't around — by choice or by circumstance? That is where God steps in. He says he'll be a father to the fatherless and a husband to the widows.

That truth has been a great source of comfort to me during times when Bob is gone. It comforts me now when we face the prospect of his being gone many months due to military conflicts around the world. It's also a source of great relief to know that God doesn't expect Bob to be me when I'm gone or expect me to be Bob when he's gone. If you are concerned that there is a gap in your child's life — when a parent is emotionally or physically not there for him or her — then you can trust God to stand in those gaps. Just ask him and he will be there for you and your child.

A *father to the fatherless, a defender of widows, is God in his holy dwelling.*

PSALM 68:5

whining or shining?

Annetta E. Dellinger

....

Joy is a choice, a matter of attitude that stems from one's confidence in God . . . that He is at work, in full control, amidst whatever has, is, or will happen.

CHARLES SWINDOLL

I'm tired, busy, and stressed. How can God expect me to wake up in the morning and find a reason to rejoice?" my daughter-in-law asked.

For the past year Libby's life could have been described as a treadmill locked in high gear with no slow-down button to push before the next crisis came along. She worked full time and on her day off was a volunteer art teacher in her younger son's Christian day school. Woven into those threads of stress were additional challenges with her prodigal older son.

Libby, a wife and homemaker, also faced the difficulty of being the sole caretaker for her mother, who in the past nine months had her leg amputated, began kidney dialysis, experienced a heart attack, and was diagnosed with cancer. Libby's phrase of the day was, "How can I rejoice when all *this* is happening?"

Our Libby had the support of a loving spouse and encouragement from family and friends, but she needed to de-stress. One day I said, "I know you've turned me down in the past, but I'd still like to take you on a mini-vacation." Finally the thought of a totally relaxing time away from her enormous pressures enticed her. Libby's "yes" surprised both of us.

After taking care of multiple family details, Libby, her younger son DJ, and I headed for the mountains. We agreed to think only positive thoughts and not call home. We were determined to make fresh memories and laugh until our sides hurt. When I thought up this grand adventure, I didn't realize I'd be the one supplying the laughter. Jumping over a split-rail fence, my shoe got caught. When it "disengaged," I fell off the fence and went into a roll. The not-too-graceful mother-in-law and grandmother landed with the picnic food among the wild flowers. I laughed until I cried.

The comic relief of that day seemed to give Libby a fresh perspective on life, but our fun didn't last. When we returned to our car and got on the road, a woman cut across three lanes of traffic and crashed into my driver's side door. Libby immediately stepped back into her caretaker role, first making sure no one was hurt and then taking care of the endless details related to the accident report on my totaled car.

Later that evening we reviewed the day — along with our blessings. As horrendous as our experience had been, none of us had whiplash. D.J., who always sat behind the driver in the backseat, was, for the first time, sitting behind the passenger. He was unharmed.

We started listing our reasons to be grateful. The police were only a block away and saw the accident happen. The tow truck driver just *happened* to suggest that his shuttle driver come along in case we needed a ride to the rental car facility. We arrived six minutes before closing time.

We agreed that we would never talk about the accident without talking about God's mercy, too. We had so many reasons to rejoice because the real joy we experienced was being *in* God's presence.

My car was totaled, but I could still treasure the memories of spending time with my dearly loved daughter-in-law and grandson. It was even fun wearing my picnic food. Remembering the smiles triggered by my not-so-graceful scramble over the split-rail fence still makes me laugh out loud.

Libby's reaction to our family adventure was my favorite: "I've come to the conclusion that what I thought would be my vacation to de-stress might have been God's way of reassuring me that his fingerprints are in *each* challenge I face. When I wake up and feel life is too hard, I realize I have a choice every day — to whine or to shine. As I think about how God's mercy embraced our getaway in the middle of an impossible situation, I'm energized to get up, grab God's joy, and go into a new day smiling."

We can't round up enough containers to hold everything God generously pours into our lives through the Holy Spirit!

ROMANS 5:5 MSG

what does love look like?

Ellie Kay

....

*For children, stories become one part road map, one part
guideline, one part pattern, one part touchstone,
and one part resource as they live out their lives and
build their families and their futures.*

BOB BENSON

*T*his is *the* most romantic movie in the world!" my
ten-year-old daughter Bethany sobbed. "Please
pass the tissues."

The movie in the video player continued. "Oh, darling! In
six months, I'll meet you at the top of the Empire State Building! I'll be there, dearest. I'll be there." Then Cary Grant took
Deborah Kerr in his arms and kissed her passionately in that
timeless classic *An Affair to Remember.*

I teared up as well, knowing that the heroine was destined
to be crippled by a taxi cab and would never make that fateful
meeting.

Our hothouse of feminine emotions was rudely interrupted
by my thirteen-year-old son. "I can't believe this! Why are you
sobbing over *that?* It's just a movie!"

I banished him to the basketball court with his three brothers. Men! They never "get" these divine movies.

But Bethany and I do. I blubbered through *Sleepless in Seattle*, especially when I thought Meg Ryan would miss Tom Hanks when he was at the top of the Empire State Building on Valentine's Day.

So when I discovered that Bob and I would be in New York City on Valentine's Day for our oldest daughter's graduation from Columbia University, I decided that Bob and I would do the Empire State Building romantic thingy.

But when I told Bob that we were going to this romantic icon, "The World's Greatest Fighter Pilot" groaned, "Do I *have* to?"

It's not that my husband is unromantic — he's just afraid of open heights. You may scoff, "A pilot who's afraid of heights? You gotta be kidding!"

But I'm not.

And he is.

"But how can you fly jets?" most people ask my husband when they hear of his phobia. To which he responds, "In a jet, I'm in control and I'm surrounded by a canopy that makes me feel like I'm inside a protective space. I'm never scared in a jet unless someone is firing missiles at me. But in open heights . . . that's a different story!"

• •

The big day arrived and I was soooo looking forward to our trip to the top of the Empire State Building. While we were waiting in line with other romantics, Bob's palms were sweaty and he kept asking, "Do I *have* to?"

We bought our tickets, walked toward the elevators, and, just as we approached the elevator doors, Bob, right on cue, sputtered, "Uh, I'm going to the bathroom. I'll meet you at the top."

You see, part of the romance (at least in the movies) is going up in separate elevators and, when he sees her at the top, he says, "I *knew* you'd be here!" They then run into each other's arms and onlookers sigh at the sweet spontaneity.

But things never work out the way they do in movies.

While I was in the elevator, I met some really nice people and we got to chatting. My friends say that I make new friends everywhere I go. As we stepped onto the 102nd floor, my newfound friends wished me well, and I went to the observation deck to wait. New York City is *very* cold in February, and the wind chill factor at the top of the Empire State Building makes it even colder. But I bundled myself in my coat and gloves and waited by the railing for my true love to arrive.

And I waited. And waited.

My nose started to run. My ears were getting cold. Still I waited.

As I wiped my reddening schnoz with a Kleenex, I began to think that Bob had wimped out. This was not the way they did it in the movies.

I was about to give up and go back down to find the "World's Greatest Flying Chicken" when I felt a tap on my shoulder. I turned around. There was Bob, shivering in his flight jacket. Sweat was running down his brow.

Mechanically (and very unromantically, I might add) he took my semi-frozen fingers into his icy palms and, with chattering teeth, muttered, "Oh. It's you. I knew you'd be here.... Can we go back down now?"

At that moment, my elevator friends approached us and I introduced them to Bob.

"Oh, we heard all about you on the elevator. How you fly the Stealth and how you're afraid of heights and how you're doing this for your wife." They smiled and offered to take our picture.

Bob smiled like a wooden boy and, through slightly gritted teeth, said, "Gee, uh ... that's great ... nice meeting you ... but I really need to go ... *now!*"

Ah, the things we do for love.

. . . .

This is a story I have told over and over to our children. It's become a family classic — with humor.

Our sons have been known to snicker and roll their eyes during the telling, but I knew they were learning an important principle of marriage without even realizing it. Bethany was always a more appreciative audience, relishing every romantic detail of our less-than-romantic meeting at the top of the Empire State Building.

I always tell the kids that even though it was hard for him, their dad made a special effort that day to do something special and romantic for me.

Over the years, our children have come to understand that their parents will go to extraordinary lengths to put romance in their marriage. They've also seen and heard our day-to-day expressions of love. They've heard us call each other "Beloved." They've been in earshot when Bob has "bragged on me" in front of our friends. They've heard him jokingly, but seriously, put boundaries on our relationship that protect our marriage. To this day, when another man gives me a hug and a social kiss on the cheek (as they do in some military circles) or a playful pat on the arm, Bob will say with a smile, "Don't touch my wife."

Children learn the most about marriage from their parents. They learn from our silly and serious stories of romancing our partner. They learn by observing the interactions that we, as moms and dads, have each day with our spouse. Being able to observe a classic tale of romance, right in their own home, makes it easier for them to develop a growing, healthy marriage relationship when they come of age and find their own true love.

. . . .

Place these words on your hearts. Get them deep inside you . . .
Teach them to your children. Talk about them wherever you are,
sitting at home or walking in the street; talk about them from the
time you get up in the morning until you fall into bed at night.

DEUTERONOMY 11:19 MSG

a view of the garden

Anne Denmark

···

*My mother's friendship has planted a little garden in my world,
and it's one of the most beautiful places I've ever seen.*

J. GEHRER

J don't know when it happened. Perhaps it was on spring walks to the old bush, hunting for pussy willows. Or was it the day a magnificent bouquet of red tulips greeted me at the kitchen table after school? Maybe it was the time the mailman delivered a large package of freshly cut cedar and pine to our new home for Christmas decorating. I don't know *when* it happened, but my mother passed down to me her love of gardening.

When Mom visited me in Oklahoma in the early spring, she would always unpack her tiny garden shoes from her suitcase. She was eager for our shared joy — the daily ritual of inspecting the gardens. Early each morning when I returned from my power walk, Mom would greet me on the back porch, coffee in hand, eager to examine every new shoot and blossom.

As we strolled through the garden, our conversation was high-lighted by what was blooming, as if flowers recorded our days and moods. Fragrances flashed us back to memories of folks we knew and loved. Together we watched God's seasonal story of new life unfolding.

One morning while we were on our usual garden rounds, I leaned down to pull a stray weed when Mom said; "Anne, I'd like to think that when I get to heaven, I could look down and see you here in the garden." This sobering comment was definitely not our usual garden chatter. It left me feeling uneasy. My thoughts would not connect. We had never spoken to each other about death. I remember thinking it was far too soon to start talking about such things.

Not knowing how to respond, I said something light-hearted. "Well, Mom, if you are ever looking for me from heaven, you'll find me here in the garden." Then we looked to see if the slugs were still eating the pansies.

My mom passed away suddenly due to respiratory failure and she's in heaven now, her gardening days cut so much shorter than either of us anticipated. From my kitchen window I see the morning sun on the fresh pink blooms of the honey-suckle vine. It was Mom's last gift to me. How appropriate that it flowers every spring at the same time she used to make her yearly visits to my home. My heart smiles as I remember how carefully she positioned the vine along the fence so it would greet me during my morning viewing of the garden.

I wonder sometimes when I am trimming the roses or watering the lilies if Mom can look down and see me. What we shared through our garden bond will always remain. All around me are fragrant reminders of our times together. I look forward to our reunion in heaven. I wonder if it will be in a garden.

There is one thing I know for certain. I am always in God's view. I am never out of his sight. I don't know *when* it happened. Perhaps it was the first time I saw tiny snow drops blooming beneath the last snow of winter. Or was it the day I marveled at the unfailing order of the seasons. Maybe it was the time I watched a busy bee coat his hairy legs with pollen from an iris. I don't know *when* it happened, but God passed on to me the knowledge that he is there even when I can't see him. It probably happened in the garden.

* * *

For since the creation of the world God's invisible qualities —
his eternal power and divine nature — have been clearly seen,
being understood from what has been made,
so that people are without excuse.

ROMANS 1:20 TNIV

the stepford children

Ellie Kay

Stick to your guns, but don't shoot yourself in the foot.

DR. KEVIN LEMAN,
MAKING CHILDREN MIND WITHOUT LOSING YOURS

*P*hilip, would you please stop arguing with Joshua?" I
asked as we were on our way to the store.

"Yes, Mom," he crooned as he obeyed. I could see
him flash an impish smile at me in the rearview mirror.

"Bethany, when we get back from the store, you're going to
need to fold that load of whites." I waited for the inevitable
protests, which started to come, then were quickly muffled by
Daniel's hand over her mouth.

"Yes, Mom, I'd be happy to do that, Mother dear," she said
politely as Daniel removed his hand and raised his eyebrows
at her.

I knew something was up. All morning, my requests had
been met with "Yes, dear Mother" or "No, I don't believe so,
Mother." I was beginning to feel I was living with the robot-like

Stepford children from a B-rated '70s movie that's been remade into a current hit.

I tried one last thing.

"Daniel, could you please practice Joshua's spelling words?" I had him now; everyone in our family would rather clean a toilet than go through the pain of that task. Even Mother Teresa would have said, "I give up on the pest!"

"Um . . . " I watched him in the mirror as the other kids began to poke him in the side. "Um . . . .sure, Mother dearest. I think he's really getting better at spelling all the time."

"That's it!" I turned off the CD so the kids could hear me. "I knew something was up. You guys are just being nice to me so I'll give PlayStation 2 back to you, aren't you?"

There was an audible round of sighs in the car. Philip's disappointed voice said, "See, I told you, Daniel. I knew she'd know what we were up to."

When we returned home, Daniel helped Joshua with his spelling words, Bethany folded the load of laundry, and Jonathan straightened his room and put away his toys.

Then they all took turns playing PlayStation 2.

. . . .

Any experienced mom will tell you that it's important to pick your battles. I took the PlayStation away from my kids after they kept violating the "one-hour rule." They knew they could only play one hour a day. Their consistent violation of that rule was leading them down a slippery slope to lethargic behavior.

I knew they'd had too much electronic stimulus when Joshua came running up to me and asked me to feel the back of his head. I thought he'd maybe fallen down and banged it or something as I felt around for a bump.

"Well," he asked, "do you feel it?"

"I don't feel anything. What happened anyway?" I was confused.

"Um." He really looked bothered. "I just played two hours of PlayStation and I was wondering if my brain was turning to mush yet."

That's when I knew it was time to remove the PS2 for a while. The lack of electronic stimulation lasted for a full month. By the time the Stepford children conspired together to try to accelerate the process, I was already about to give back their privileges. This was a battle line I'd drawn and re-evaluated. Dr. Kevin Leman says, "If you're getting the idea that a different decision would be wiser or fairer, you can change your mind."*

There are other battle lines we draw with our children that we can't back down on. That's why it's important to choose battles wisely. For example, you probably won't want to back down on knowing who your children's friends are and what kind of

---

* Kevin Leman, *Making Your Children Mind Without Losing Yours* (Grand Rapids, Mich.: Revell, 2000), 21

television shows they're watching. But you can have a "questionable" friend over to your home so your family can be an influence on them rather than allow your child to go to that friend's home. Or, you can read a review of a movie they want to see and, if you're watching a video, fast-forward through the unacceptable scenes. These are ways to turn a win-lose battle into a victory for everyone involved.

As far as my Stepford children go, they still get only one hour of PlayStation on their day of the week. After all, I don't want their brains to turn to mush.

You will not have to fight this battle. Take up your positions; stand firm and see the deliverance the LORD will give you. . . . Do not be afraid; do not be discouraged.

2 CHRONICLES 20:17

my wild, wacky, warmhearted
mother-in-law

Carol Kent

··

Lord, let me never enter a life, except to build.

LILA TROTMAN,
QUOTED FROM A CHINA PLATE FOUND IN A GIFT SHOP

*I*t was the spring of 1969. Gene (my fiancé) and I were graduating from college in late May, and we were enthusiastically making plans for a summer wedding. Gene was gradually meeting my relatives, and I was meeting his extended family. *That was a real trip!* Everything about his family was different from my family — the way we set the table, the way we decorated our homes, the way we did our reunions — but the other big difference was the *people!*

It was time for me to meet Gene's grandparents, and as we drove to their country home, I was anticipating a lovely afternoon with a mild-mannered elderly couple. As we walked in the door, Gene hugged his grandparents and briefly introduced me as his soon-to-be bride.

Grandpa was rather intimidating at six feet, two inches in height, and he walked directly to my side, pulled my chin up so he could look me squarely in the face, and within spittin' range he loudly proclaimed, "So this is Eugene's girlfriend!" He promptly licked his lips and plastered me with a kiss that was so intense I'm sure I turned bright red from head to foot.

That visit was the first of many opportunities of getting to know Gene's side of the family. All of them were interesting — and many could provide fodder for a scintillating novel. However, getting to know Gene's mom — my future mother-in-law — was the most fascinating experience of all. Mom had a hard life; she worked in a battery factory for years to put food on the table and to help keep the family afloat financially. She was a trailblazer in the women's "equal pay for equal work" endeavor at her place of employment long before she knew there was a movement called women's liberation. Mom could "hold her own" with the boys who worked in the plant, and she was a captivating conversationalist.

She had not come from a rigid religious background, and her speech was a bit "salty," when compared with the strict Christian upbringing I had known. Mom loved to tell humorous stories about her life experiences, and the one we heard most often was about the day she and Gene's father went to a wrestling match where they had purchased ringside seats. Brute Bernard, a renowned wrestler in his day, got thrown out of the ring. While still outside the ring, standing near Gene's mother,

Brute made some moves that made Mom mad. She stood to her feet and whacked him with her purse.

That was Mom — you never had to guess where she was coming from because she told you. I admired that about her. She didn't play games about how she felt about anybody, but I wondered how I would ever fit into this family that was so different from mine.

Gene and I married that July, and we took up residence in a former funeral home — it was cheap and we needed inexpensive lodging. One day when I was in the kitchen with my mother-in-law, she told me that when she was seventeen, she found herself pregnant and unmarried. Her mother was furious with her for being an unwed pregnant teenager — a disgrace to the entire family.

On the day her baby was born, she was holding her newborn when her mother walked into the room. She looked at her daughter, gazed down at the infant in her arms, and looked up again at her daughter. Then in a sarcastic tone she said, "For the last nine months I prayed that this baby would be born dead!" She pivoted on her heel and marched out of the room.

I felt weak in the knees and faint in the heart. The baby my mother-in-law was holding is the man I'm married to today — a funny, uplifting, giving, encouraging, dynamic, and intelligent husband who has blessed my life in countless ways. I realized if Grandma had gotten her wish, I would have missed out on a spectacular spouse.

That day God gave me new eyes to see the distinctive beauty of my mother-in-law. I instantly realized she could have allowed that cruel remark from her mother to fill her with bitterness, anger, unforgiveness, and self-pity. But instead, she forgave her mother and used the "tough stuff" of her life as a platform for developing her gift of compassion for others.

Her mother grew to love the grandchild she thought she didn't want. But the most powerful life lesson in this experience has been watching my mother-in-law demonstrate unconditional love, acts of kindness, and undeserved mercy in her relationships with others. She spent many years caring for the needs of mentally challenged adults. Mom also has been a remarkable grandmother to our son.

Yes, my mother-in-law *is* different from *my* mother, but she has a unique beauty, wisdom, character, communication style, and zest for life that have made her one of my favorite people in the whole world. By the way, if you need a little humor to spice up your next party, invite Mom. You'll need no other form of entertainment.

God, make a fresh start in me,
shape a Genesis week from the chaos of my life.

PSALM 51:10 MSG

girls' day jammin'

Jill Lynnele Gregory

. . . .

*Tradition is not just what we receive,
it is what we create with our own hands and then hand over,
the ties we make with past and future.*

Marcia Falk

*M*y mom has often said, "I never thought when I gave birth to my children I would be giving birth to my best friends." It's true. The three sisters in our family love to spend time with our mom. Now that we are out of the house and married, we have started the tradition of having a "Girls' Day Out" during our kids' school vacation breaks.

On one day during each break we get together for lunch, or to shop at an outlet mall, or to catch a movie. No matter what the occasion, one thing is certain — we laugh and giggle until tears stream down our faces. It's a "sister-bonding time."

When my brother was married last year, we were excited for our new sister-in-law to join us. We wondered what it would be like to add another sister to our close family circle. Our mom prayed a long time for the right wife for our brother, and she made a promise to love his wife as her own daughter when that prayer was answered. Laura has been worth the wait.

One of our first opportunities to include Laura in the family tradition was at our "Girls' Day Jammin'" gathering, which always takes place on the first Saturday after school is out for the summer. That year we arrived early in the morning at my parents' house to make our family's special strawberry and triple-berry jams. The finished product produces jams for each of our families and enough extra jams that they can be used as gifts for our neighbors and for our children's teachers during the holidays.

As we entered the house with boxes of jelly jars and bags of sugar under each arm, we knew Mom had been up for hours preparing for our day. The smell of flavored coffee greeted us at the door, and Grandma's antique teacups were set out next to the coffee pot. On the stove Mom had the largest pot ever made by man, and it was gurgling with the boiling water needed to heat the jelly jars. The kitchen counter was filled with even more bags of sugar and bountiful trays of beautiful ripe berries. In addition to all of the jammin' ingredients, mom had many of our favorite foods on the dining room table so we could munch, take breaks, and have fun throughout the day.

Making jam is hard work, and each sister has a special assignment in that process. Our assembly line consists of washing the berries, cutting the stems, and crushing the fruit. Then someone measures and pours the sugar and pectin into the mixture. The jam has to be stirred as it cooks on the stove, and the jars and lids have to be heated to just the right temperature. In the past, each sister chose her favorite part of this process, and it became "her specific job" for the jammin' tradition each year.

When our sister-in-law Laura arrived, she was met with a hug and kiss from Mom. We observed and listened as our mother said, "Laura, let me show you *your* job today." She gently took Laura by the arm and led her to the kitchen. Then she trained her in the job of stirring the jam as it boils on the stove. It is the most crucial step in the process of making jam, and it's the job our mother always had in the past. We watched Mom graciously step aside to make our newest sister feel like she had always been a part of our tradition.

As we worked the rest of the day, the four sisters got caught up on each other's lives, laughed out loud, and acted flat-out silly. Before the day was half over, we knew we had been waiting for Laura all along to complete our Girls' Day Jammin' tradition.

Our mom taught us by example to open our hearts and lives to others. With her humble, sweet spirit she reached out to make Laura feel included and to let her know she is a vital part of our family. It really does take *four* sisters and a mom to make the sweetest jam.

A good woman is hard to find, and worth far more than dia-
monds. . . . She's up before dawn . . . organizing her day. . . .
When she speaks she has something worthwhile to say,
and she always says it kindly. She keeps an eye on everyone
in her household, and keeps them all busy and productive.
Her children respect and bless her.

PROVERBS 31:10, 15, 26–28 MSG

mom's rules

Ellie Kay

*Sometime . . . a wave of light breaks into our darkness,
and it is as though a voice were saying: "You are accepted."*

PAUL TILLICH

*J*ulia's mom lets *her* wear lipstick and shave her legs!"
wailed eleven-year-old Bethany, trying to make the
same point for the third time in three days.

My response was the same: "That may be *her* mother's rule,
but *my* rules are different."

Have you ever thought about the "family rules" that you
grew up with? They were probably unique to your family. There
may have even been some rules you vowed you'd never impose
in your own home. Some rules are good, but other rules deserve
to be replaced.

It's a good exercise to sit back and think of those childhood
rules. Then, fast-forward to today and think about what your
kids would say about your rules. Below is a list of the Kay family rules, complete with "Emergency Code Words" that my hus-

band and I use to prompt our kids to remember them. This gives them a chance to change their response before we have to take action.

- We love and accept you no matter how you perform. We don't always like what you do, but we always love you.
- If you're not grateful for what you get, you get nothing at all. (Emergency Code Words: Are you ungrateful?)
- It's better to tell the truth and take your medicine than to lie and get a double dose.
- If you don't like our decision, we'll listen to your side.
- At the dinner table, you will act as if you were raised in a home, not a barn.
- You never use the word *fart*. You will say "pass gas." (Emergency Code Words: What did you say?)
- If you complain about the work we've asked you to do, then you will have more work added to it. (Emergency Code Words: Are you complaining?)
- When we ask you a question or ask you to do something, you will reply with "Yes, Mama" or "Yes, Papa."
- When we do something wrong, we'll ask you for your forgiveness.

A lot of our rules are radically different from the rules I grew up with. Keep in mind that my parents were from a different time and culture, which accounts for the reason some of the rules were different. Here were a few of their rules:

- Keep the fork in your right hand and the knife in your left, both in clear sight.
- If you say the wrong thing at the dinner table, you will get bopped in the head.
- Instant tea and instant mashed potatoes (newly discovered upon arrival in America) will take precedence over brewed tea and real potatoes.
- If you make a comment about the mashed potatoes, you will get bopped in the head.
- He who yells loudest at the dinner table will be heard.
- No one eats Grandma's Kellogg's Corn Pops or you know what will happen.
- Eggplant will be eaten and enjoyed on a regular basis, and you will thank Grandma for growing two acres of it in her garden.
- If you perform well, you will be accepted.
- Twelve-year-old girls shouldn't ride on minibikes with their girlfriends or their grandma will chase them up and down the street with a broom. (I finally decided to stop riding the minibike after this happened a dozen times.)

Written and unwritten rules are what make up the fabric of a home. Some are learned from the previous generation, and they are not necessarily *good* rules — but are perpetuated anyway. In my family of origin a high value was placed on performance, and the rule list never ended. I wanted to be accepted, so I performed by bringing home straight A's, winning outstanding bandsman, and earning a college scholarship.

When I grew up and had a family of my own, I changed some of the rules. For example, we eat the American way, with one hand politely in the lap and the other holding the fork. In Spain, they'd ask, "What are you doing with that hand in your lap?" But here, it's considered good table manners.

You may be a mom who grew up with parents who handed down a legacy of emotional and physical pain. It's okay, and necessary, to break that generational cycle. Changing the rules doesn't mean you're dishonoring your parents; it means you're giving your kids a fresh start.

The good news is that God has given you power to break free from a negative pattern to become the kind of parents that he has planned for you to be. Even if those who are supposed to love you the most have ended up hurting you the worst, you are still accepted in Christ Jesus and can have victory over the past. That's more than a rule — it's a promise!

. . . .

Can a mother forget the baby at her breast and have no compassion on the child she has borne? Though she may forget, I will not forget you! See, I have engraved you on the palms of my hands.

ISAIAH 49:15 – 16

proud and prejudiced

Joy Carlson

. . . .

The pride of youth is in strength and beauty,
the pride of old age is in discretion.

DEMOCRITUS

I have been mature for my age since the day I was born. At least that's what everyone has always told me. Of course, I come from a family who knows how to lay it on pretty thick when it comes to compliments of any kind.

"Oh, Joy, you are so clever and creative!"

"Isn't she the cutest thing you've ever seen?"

"She's so talented!"

"You certainly have wisdom beyond your years."

You get the picture. I had pretty healthy self-esteem and I rather enjoyed having the people in my life exaggerate my value and attributes as a young woman.

. . . .

Then came the day my future husband introduced me to his mother. He and I walked side by side to the library where she worked on the campus of the college we were attending. Apparently he had prepared her for this introduction before I arrived.

"Mom, I'm bringing someone over here I want you to meet. Her name is Joy Afman."

"Who *is* she?" my future mother-in-law inquired.

"She's the girl I'm going to marry."

With that groundwork thoroughly laid, we approached the building and entered confidently. Introductions were made, but something was missing. I sensed an attitude of polite reservation.

Ah, well, I thought, *this is probably to be expected. After all, we're getting married a little suddenly.* I was convinced that once she came to appreciate my charming personality and my generous endowment of wisdom, any prejudices she had toward me would fade. I would easily win her over. Admittedly, eighteen was a little young to get engaged, but I was such a *mature* eighteen. I smugly thought: *She will one day realize her family was blessed to have me become part of it!*

At one point during our six-month engagement I began a new college course and needed a place to board. My future mother-in-law opened her home to me. This was my first opportunity to witness the gracious gifts of giving and service she possessed. Unfortunately, at the time I saw it more as an opportunity to convince her I was the right girl for her son. I lived in the home for almost two months — with my future mother- and father-in-law and a younger daughter they were still raising — and I took her gracious hospitality for granted.

After my husband and I were married, we began our family — and it grew quickly. I gave birth to a son, followed by a daughter; the years flew by as three more sons were born, followed by a second daughter, and then another baby boy. Seven children make for a busy household and a lot of responsibility. Mom was always there when we needed anything and intentionally out of the way when we didn't. When we were struggling in our marriage, she was a big part of the glue that held us together.

. . . .

As the years rolled by, I saw a bigger picture — a picture that for once didn't have *me* as the central theme. I realized that my initial feelings of being unaccepted or unappreciated by my mother-in-law were really just a selfish demand that she set me up on a pedestal and flatter me with the words I was so accustomed to hearing in earlier years.

Instead of expecting her to meet my personal requirements of perfection, I began to appreciate her *more* because she was so different from me. She often asked:

"How can I help?"

"What do you need?"

"Would you like me to bring anything when I come over?"

These are the words most often spoken to me by my mother-in-law. For our oldest son's graduation open house, she not only baked 1,000 cookies but also spent two days working side by side with me preparing, serving, and cleaning up after an enormous celebration. We still have six school-age children, and when Mom comes to take care of our little ones for several days at a time, I can leave home with my mind completely at ease because I know she will lay down her every need to make sure her grandchildren are happy, well fed, and living in an orderly environment.

Oh, yes, there is something good to be said for words of praise and affirmation. I thrive on them. But I feel incredibly blessed to have a mother-in-law who loved me enough to put up with my pride and arrogance so she could show me by her quiet example the nature of a true servant's mature and humble heart.

....

Fear-of-GOD is a school in skilled living — first you learn humility, then you experience glory.

PROVERBS 15:33 MSG

money matters

Ellie Kay

....

You spend a billion here, you spend a billion there.
Sooner or later it adds up to real money.

SENATOR EVERETT DIRKSEN

ut *why* do we have to pay for half of our T-shirts?" wailed Bethany as an eight-year-old. "Why don't you just write a check?"

"Yeah, Mama!" echoed five-year-old Joshua passionately, who was dressed up in his cowboy outfit. "You gots lots of money in dat check thing!" He peeked at me from under the rim of his cowboy hat.

Bethany was elected to present the case on behalf of her disgruntled constituents (her four brothers), who now stood behind her in an uncharacteristic show of support.

Her courage grew as she continued, "We really want those Kovenant Kids shirts so we can wear them to club. Everyone else is going to get them." She looked over at her brother Philip.

On cue, Philip changed tactics and tried the spiritual approach. "We could even wear them out in public and be a Christian witness. When people ask us about our shirts, we could tell them God loves them!"

I was obviously the target of a carefully planned conspiracy.

I put my hands on my hips and repeated myself for the second time, "I already said that we would pay for half of your T-shirts. You guys will take better care of those shirts and they'll mean more to you if you earn a portion for their purchase."

There arose a low moan, as if the Grinch had just announced there would be no Christmas this year. They knew that when their mom started quoting the Bill of Rights, there would be no more debate.

Wagging my pointy Grinchy finger, I drove home the point: "If you're not grateful for half, then you can have *nothing*." I smoothed Joshua's bangs as he looked at me with sad eyes. "We'll give you jobs to earn the money."

As they realized defeat, the murmuring crowd dispersed. I overheard Daniel grumble, "Next time, we'll get Joshua to ask her — he's the baby of the family."

For days, the older kids did odd jobs and earned quarters toward the $4 portion of their $8 shirts. Poor Joshua was always a day late or a dollar short — the other kids did the work before he had a chance to do anything.

One afternoon he came running through the house muttering, "I'm gonna *earn* that money!"

I found him rummaging through the dress-up box. Then he ran into the garage and got the wagon. He ran back inside and enlisted his sister's help with a sign before darting outside again. In one of his turbo runs, I heard him repeat determinedly, "I'm going to *earn* that money!"

Then things got suspiciously quiet. When I went outside to see what my industrious baby was up to, my heart just melted. Joshua was sitting by the side of the driveway in a lawn chair with his red wagon in front of him. He had on his cowboy hat and favorite blue, orange, and yellow striped shorts. Over his red shirt was a bright multicolored Mexican vest with a sheriff's badge pinned neatly on it — upside down. Around his waist he sported a Roy Rogers holster with shiny plastic silver guns and a blue bandanna. The crowning touch of this Tex-Mex ensemble was a pair of cowboy boots. The boots and shorts combo made him look like a Texas hick vacationing in Puerto Vallarta. A pair of lime green sunglasses completed the outfit as he awaited business. The sign taped to the wagon read: "COWBOY AUTOGRAPHS — 10 cents."

When I saw my little guy sitting out in the 105-degree heat of a New Mexico summer, my mama's heart went out to him. The only person out in that kind of heat was the mail carrier (who had already made her rounds), and I was pretty sure she was all stocked up on cowboy autographs. Watching my pint-sized John Wayne sit out there, full of hope, was just too much for me. So I got in line and bought forty autographs.

I wonder if the way I saw my little boy is the way God sometimes looks at us — with a heart full of compassion. Have you ever thought of God looking at you as you look at your children's efforts to get a job done? God sees you plugging along in life, trying to get a better grip on your finances, or mothering skills, or just living life, and he's eager to meet us where we are. I told Joshua that I still wanted him to do the job he had set out to do, so he dutifully scrawled out "J-o-s-h-u-a" forty times.

God knows your past failures, he knows your current limitations — but he also knows your heart. If you want to be a good steward of everything you have and teach your kids to be the same, then you can be confident that God will send you the resources you need to accomplish that worthy goal.

* * *

Some give freely, yet grow all the richer;
others withhold what is due, and only suffer want.

PROVERBS 11:24 NRSV

military mom

Shirley Carter Liechty

There were days when we would say, "Lord, could you just show us that you love us?" Then something extraordinary would happen. . . . We thought of those things as the Lord saying, "I'm still here."

GRACIA BURNHAM

I t should have been the most exotic trip of my life. My husband and I were in a small five-passenger boat on a river winding through the tropical rainforest of Ecuador. A missionary friend was serving as our guide. The natural beauty of the jungle and my rising fears made strange companions. My mind swirled and my stomach churned.

I'm in a boat on a river and I don't swim.

I'm deathly afraid of snakes.

Drug dealers are known to pass through this area.

I pushed aside thoughts of immanent danger and postponed indulging my emotions. My fears were not primarily of snakes, the water, or even the drug dealers, but of something much more ominous.

A few days before, the dreaded news had reached us by phone that our nineteen-year old son, Todd, was being deployed to Saudi Arabia to take part in the Gulf War. Hanging up the receiver, I mechanically shared the news with my husband and our missionary friends. I tried to control my emotions, knowing our purpose in being there was to encourage *them*. We continued with the rest of our trip as planned.

A week later we were home, and I allowed myself to face my fears and to feel the emotions of being a military mom. It was now six weeks before Christmas. Agonizing in prayer, my mind raced from one thought to another. I knew there were other mothers like me — praying mothers. They had prayed for their children when they were sent on overseas missions, but their sons or daughters did not come back.

My mind raced back to my struggle with infertility. I relived the agonizing months as we waited to adopt this child. I thought about the years of nurturing my son and keeping him safe from on-coming traffic, dangerous medications, and other childhood perils. Now my son was going to war and I was powerless to protect him.

My faith seemed small, and my need was great. I was shaking with fear. In the silence I cried: *Please, God, please help me not to fail you. I can't bear to lose him. Don't let him die far away with no one to hold him.* My pillow was wet with tears, and my prayer dissolved into groans.

Then, as clearly as in an audible voice, God spoke to me, "I know . . . I had a Son."

I was startled, and the words took my breath away. As God's Spirit stirred within me, years of past Bible teaching flashed through my mind: *Yes! God understood my pain! He understood my love! God was a parent who had suffered separation and loss, and even the death of his Son!* I stopped weeping, and I grew quiet and peaceful. The Comforter was there. I had a quiet confidence that I could trust God with my son.

A week later, Todd called home asking me to send him a list of what his dad and I wanted for Christmas. I wrote back, mentioning something to do with baseball for his dad. I didn't know what to suggest for me, but I had recently been fascinated with some lovely porcelain carousels in the mall gift shops. I jotted "carousel horse" on the list and dropped the letter in the mail.

During the first week of December 1990 we had a day of celebration. Todd came, and we hastily chose a date when we could have our family Christmas dinner and gift exchange. When I opened my gift from Todd, I unwrapped an exquisite musical carousel in soft pastel colors. I carefully wound it and listened to its tender melody. By now I was teary-eyed.

Through my sniffling, I heard Todd's somewhat apologetic words, "Mom, I didn't know what to get you. Do you like it?" Stunned, I listened as he explained that he had never received the letter with my suggestions for Christmas gifts — even though it had been mailed two weeks earlier! Today my carousel horse remains one of my most prized possessions — a treasured gift from my son and an unforgettable reminder of the time God chose to remind me of his love and steadfast presence during a fearful experience in my life.

* * *

So do not fear, for I am with you; do not be dismayed,
for I am your God. I will strengthen you and help you;
I will uphold you with my righteous right hand.

ISAIAH 41:10

chick flicks and time travel

Ellie Kay

....

*A Minnesota town with a volunteer fire department has this slogan,
"We'll know where we're going when we get there."*

CHARLES SWINDOLL

*I*f you haven't seen the remake of the classic movie
Father of the Bride, run — don't walk — to the nearest
rental store. Actually, the original, starring Elizabeth
Taylor and Spencer Tracy, as well as the remake, starring Steve
Martin and Diane Keaton, should be required viewing for all
brides-to-be *and* moms-to-be. And since this *is* partly my book —
you are required to see these movies.

In the new version, there's a priceless scene where the
daughter first tells her dad she's engaged. She has just recently
returned from a trip to Rome and she's sitting at the dinner table
with her family as she struggles to explain:

"You see, I met this guy . . . and he's completely wonderful.
He's a lot like Dad, actually. Well, we fell in love and . . . we've

decided to get married." Her countenance glows with the wonder of it all as she exclaims, "I'm engaged! Ahhh! Can you believe it? I'm getting married!" She wiggles in her seat like a giddy school girl.

At this point, George Banks looks at his daughter and does a double take. Instead of seeing his adult daughter, he sees his seven-year-old little girl, with brown pigtails and red ribbons in her hair. She speaks to him in an angelic voice, "Dad, I met a man in Rome and he's wonderful and he's brilliant and we're getting married."

When this movie first came out on video, Bethany was about five years old. One day shortly after Bob and I had seen the movie, I braided Bethany's hair so that she looked like the little girl in the movie. I thought I would have a little fun at Bob's expense. That night, when he came home from work, Bethany sat at the dinner table and on my silent cue announced with sincerity, "Papa, I met a man in Rome, we fell in love, and I'm going to get married."

It was soooo cute that I just knew Bob would love how sweetly Bethany could reenact that scene. Well, I found out I didn't know Bob as well as I thought!

When Bethany said her line, Bob put down his fork and looked up in bewilderment. The expression on his face indicated that his mind was fast-forwarding about twenty years — and he didn't like what he saw: his precious little "Bunny" all grown up and leaving her papa. He shuddered at the thought and shook his bewildered head as he groused, "That's *not* funny. That's not funny at all."

. . . .

I may be stretching it a bit, but I believe there can be some real value in chick flicks for our kids and for us. For one thing, the episode I just described with Bob was a watershed moment that helped me to do a little time travel of my own. When my kids were young and engaged in one mess after another, I'd think about what it would be like when they were teenagers. I would try to relish those baby and preschool years, knowing they would pass faster than Marty could go from zero to eighty-eight miles per hour in *Back to the Future*. Well, that movie wasn't a "chick flick," but it did teach me a lesson about the swift passage of time.

There's something else that is great about chick flicks: if you start your kids on them while they're young, they will think that a movie isn't any good unless it makes Mama cry. That's right. Our kids have seen so many chick flicks that they can quote lines (and often do) from *Singing in the Rain*, *Seven Brides for Seven Brothers*, *Sleepless in Seattle* (I fast-forward a few scenes in that one), and *It's a Wonderful Life*. My boys recognize Jimmy Stewart in an instant and don't know who Brad Pitt is.

Ah . . . I know what you're thinking — that I'm raising a bunch of mama's boys, right? Well, I'm not. My sons can get in there and tussle with the best of teenaged boys, but they also are learning, primarily from chick flicks, that women are different. Girls cry over things that make them sad. My sons delight in girlie things, and that's all right. Just because women are different doesn't make them bad — it makes them special. I would give a few more rationalizations for forcing my kids to watch chick flicks instead of the latest *Star Wars* movie, but I think that's about all the time and space I have right now. Besides, I just bought *Sense and Sensibility*, and my boys are calling me to get off the computer and come into the living room so we can start the flick.

· ·

I love those who love me, and those who seek me find me.

PROVERBS 8:17

praise power

Bonnie Afman Emmorey

Praise God even when you don't understand what He is doing.

HENRY JACOBSEN

*Y*es, Dad had always been the rock of the family, but Mother was the one we turned to when we needed comfort or nurturing. She was always there for us. She nursed each one of us through all the childhood diseases; she cried with us over boyfriend troubles; she taught us biblically based values. I knew that I could call Mother any time of the day or night, and it would be as if she were *expecting* my call.

Now it was my turn. Mother had called to let me know that Dad was going into the hospital the next day for emergency heart bypass surgery. I knew I couldn't let her face that event alone. I made arrangements for my family and drove four hours to meet Mother at the hospital. That night we stayed in the hospital guesthouse, but neither of us slept. What if—? We couldn't even say it out loud, but it was on our hearts and minds.

We had a time of prayer with Dad before they wheeled him away, but it didn't give us any peace. Encouraging words were spoken, but we were not encouraged. We went to the cafeteria for coffee; we played games in the waiting room; we wandered the hospital halls; we waited and we agonized.

Our steps led us to the hospital chapel. It was not my idea of what a chapel should be. From my limited experience, hospital chapels were always small, dim, and solemn. This was a large room with windows covering one wall. It was painted bright yellow and the sun was streaming in. It was a happy room.

Once again, Mother and I prayed together for Dad, for the doctors, for the nurses and other assistants, for the equipment. I believe we covered every possible detail, but still we had no peace.

As we sat there, our fears were taking over and anxiety started controlling our every thought. Quietly Mother said, "Bonnie, you know there is *power* in praise. Let's sing. Let's sing praises to our Lord." There were songbooks in the chapel, and we opened them at the first page and started singing. We sang from the depths of our hearts. We are both altos, but we made a joyful noise. We sang every praise song in the book.

No one else came in, so we felt no self-consciousness. Before long our hearts began to lift. It was the most amazing experience. When we left that chapel, we both had the peace that passes all understanding — the peace of God.

The day suddenly seemed to be flying by even though the surgery went two hours longer than expected. When it was finally over, they let us go in and see Dad. Two of my sisters arrived and they went in first. As they walked out, they had tears streaming down their faces and could only comment on how terrible Dad looked.

Then it was our turn. Mother and I went in, looked at Dad all bloated and swollen with body fluids, and all we could do was grin at each other. We were almost giddy. He looked awful, but he was alive! The surgery was a success and praises were on our lips.

Thirteen years later Mother called with similar news. Dad was back in the hospital and the doctors were not giving her much hope. After a second heart bypass surgery, a staph infection had set in and much damage had been done to his lungs. On Thanksgiving Day the family gathered at the hospital. Two by two, we were allowed to see Dad and say our good-byes.

Earlier, Mother had let us all know that she was not about to leave Dad for our traditional dinner in one of our homes. But we still *needed* to be together. She asked me to try to arrange for a place for us to have dinner as close to the hospital as possible. I finally found a hotel that assured me of a private dining room, knowing that we would need a bit of privacy for our sharing at the end of that annual meal. One by one, each family member verbalizes the blessings and challenges he or she has experienced during the course of the past year.

We arrived at the hotel only to find *their* idea of private and *my* idea of private were two different things. We were in a hotel ballroom filled with occupied tables and a long buffet line. After dinner, our sharing became a much quieter affair. Many tears were shed as each family member spoke, realizing our father was in a nearby hospital fighting for his life.

Mother was last and when she finished, there were no dry eyes. With a hushed voice, she asked if we could quietly sing "To God Be the Glory." It's the way we always close our Thanksgiving sharing time. With whispered voices we began to sing. Little by little, our voices gained strength, and by the end of the song, many of the diners in that vast ballroom were looking in our direction. It didn't matter. Praise was required. Praise was needed. Praise was the answer. As we got ready to leave, several people gathered at our table and thanked us. Praise was what they needed, too.

Later that afternoon, we heard the news. Dad's condition had changed. The doctors were amazed — he was going to pull through. Mother called it a praise miracle. It was.

. . . .

Let the whole world bless our God and sing aloud his praises.
Our lives are in his hands, and he keeps our feet from stumbling.

PSALM 66:8–9 NLT

projectiles

Ellie Kay

· ·

A friend is a gift you give yourself.

ROBERT LOUIS STEVENSON

J’ve always been a highly relational woman; that’s why my inner circle of girlfriends is priceless to me. As moms, it’s sometimes hard to find and nurture those kindred spirit friendships. God has always been faithful to either keep me connected to the friends of my past or to give me new friends in the present.

Last month it was time for a good old-fashioned chick chat with Gracie, my friend from Texas. The key to any good chick time is to let each chick have adequate time to chirp. We connected by phone and I listened to Gracie’s exciting news about the beautiful cover of her new book and was thrilled for her. I had to tune out the goings-on of my five kids, who were running in and out of the room, yelling and talking. As it turned out, I was a little *too* focused on the conversation and not focused *enough* on Joshua.

Joshua had come into the room and began rummaging through a tall, deep Adirondack basket where we throw some misplaced toys to keep them out of sight. He emptied the entire contents on the floor as I shared Gracie's joy. I saw Joshua out of the corner of my eye, but didn't really *see* him as he picked up something that interested him. It was an airplane launcher — the kind where you take a plastic airplane, put it on the long rubber band, hold the metal handle tight, and then let it fly. The only problem was, there weren't any jets around for him to launch.

So Joshua decided to use my foot. As I jabbered with Gracie, he walked across the room, sat by the end of the couch where my leg dangled off, and put the rubber band around my foot. I was somewhat aware of my son's actions, but my mind was mostly in the world of intense chick chat. He pulled the metal handle back as far as he could, with the rubber band still securely wrapped around my foot. When he had it pulled back as tight as it would go, he let go of the metal handle.

"Varoom!"

The handle traveled three feet at about 30 mph and hit the bony edge of my foot with an intensity that made me drop the phone mid-sentence.

"Oh! Oh! OOOOUCH!! Oh! Oh!!"

I couldn't talk. I could only cry out in pain. Joshua hightailed it out of the room, and the other kids came running to find their mom lying on the floor, holding her foot and fighting back tears of pain.

"What's wrong, Mama?" Jonathan cried, frightened.

"Should I call the ambulance?" asked the ever practical Philip.

"Oh! Oh! Waaa . . . Naaa . . . Oh!" was the only response I could muster.

Every time I tried to talk, the combination of the pain and the hilarity of the event would render me speechless. From the other room, Joshua shouted, "I'm sorry, Mama! It was an accident!"

Poor Gracie was still on the phone, listening to the ruckus and wondering if she should call 9-1-1. When I finally calmed down enough to get back to the phone, my words came out in such a jumble that Gracie asked in her no-nonsense way, "Ellie are you laughing, crying, or both?"

"Yes!"

First, there is only *one* bony area of my body (my feet), and Joshua's projectile knocked the fool out of it, so I was physically hurting from that. Second, I had actually sat there and *watched him do it*! I mean, talk about the "spirit of stupid" coming down all over me!

Later, when Bob asked Joshua what motivated him to do that to his mama, his answer was the typical response of a seven-year-old boy, "I just wanted to see what would happen."

Isn't life like that for us sometimes? Do you ever get so intent on the crisis du jour or the distraction of the moment that you miss the indicators of harm beaming right across your path? Maybe you've seen this in other moms: the mom who is so busy volunteering that she no longer cooks dinner for her family. Or the taxi-cab mom who is so distracted by the kids in the car that she forgets to smile and tell them she loves them as she drops them off. The working mother who gets so jazzed about a major promotion that she misses the opportunity to praise her son for his first 100 on a spelling test.

It's important to be on the lookout for the danger indicators of a family approaching critical mass in schedules, materialism, and worldliness, and needing to slow down and take a time out. A good way to keep focus is to spend daily time with God, read his Word, and pray on a regular basis. By focusing on him, you are better equipped to avoid some of the projectiles the enemy hurls your way. God may not be someone "with skin on" like a girlfriend, but he's always there and he's wiser than any chick we know.

* *

The prudent see danger and take refuge,
but the simple keep going and suffer for it.

PROVERBS 27:12

mama needs a time out!

Ellie Kay

. . . .

To forgive means to write it off. Let it go. Tear up the account.
It is to render the account "canceled."

DR. HENRY CLOUD AND DR. JOHN TOWNSEND

*I*t had been one of those days.

Bethany was a new baby, Philip was not yet a two-year-old, and Daniel was four. Bob was off flying in the final days of the Gulf War. The single mom thing wasn't going well, and I was stressed to the max. My neighbor Patti called to chat, and I was relieved for the break from changing diapers and cleaning up various messes the boys got into.

As we were talking, giggling noises wafted from the back of the house and I sensed an investigation would be prudent. I put Patti on hold and set the phone down on the cradle. Daniel and Philip were in the hallway, covered with chocolate that they dug out of my private stash, and they were playing what they dubbed "Banana Smush" with the overripe bananas I was saving to make bread.

That was the last straw.

I put my hands on my hips and shouted, "Go in the other room. I don't even want to look at you right now!"

I began to clean up the mess, forgetting about Patti hanging on the line. It only took a couple of minutes to realize that something more substantial than a dishrag was needed to get the remnants of the smush party off the floor. Anger and frustration along with a sense of injustice at being left alone with the kids welled up in me. My anger grew with every stomp of my foot down the hallway toward the kitchen.

Philip met me with a guilty look on his face and instantly became the target of my anger.

"How *could* you do this?" I shouted. "Why do you make these messes all the time?" I directed my next screams to Daniel, whom I couldn't see. "Daniel! You should know better!"

I breathed in deeply, my anger spent, while Philip looked up with large tears in his eyes. As I turned the corner to go into the kitchen, there stood Daniel, holding the phone and "chatting" with Patti.

I took it from him. "Uh, Patti? Sorry you were left on the phone there. Um, there was a little problem here."

"Yeah," she said, "I heard."

That's the way things usually work for me. When I blow it (scream, act unkindly, etc.) I usually get caught. Then there's a choice: I can either defend the actions (I was tired, Bob is gone, the kids were asking for it) or confess it and call it what it is — sin.

There are four words a lot of children never hear from their parents, but Bob and I were determined ours would hear from us: *Will you forgive me?* There are many adult children who are *still* waiting to hear those words. I know I am. Sometimes parents will get close and say, "Well, I guess I blew it," but that's not the same. No, the right response is: "Will you forgive me?"

There are few memories more humbling than what happened after my tirade on the day of the Banana Smush party. I got down on my knees, to be on eye level with Daniel and Philip, and said, "Mommy was wrong to scream. Will you forgive me for yelling at you?" Then we all prayed to Jesus and, right in front of my sons, I asked God to forgive me. Oh yeah, and I had to call Patti and ask her forgiveness as well.

It would be great to say that was the last time I blew it with my kids — but it's not. I fail on a regular basis. Sometimes I cut my teen off mid-sentence, yell, or have a bad attitude. But I always try to apologize to my kids.

Have you ever apologized to your children when you've blown it? Even the simplest apology sets the tone for an attitude of grace and forgiveness — something your children will remember when they're grown and have kids of their own.

Sometimes it's hard to admit when you're wrong, but it's imperative that your children see you model this humble posture so that they will learn how to ask for and grant forgiveness.

. . . .

If a brother or sister sins, go and point out the fault,
just between the two of you alone. If they listen to you,
you have won them over.

MATTHEW 18:15

a tale of two manicures

Jeanne Zornes

. . . .

*My mother's hands are soft, warm, and comforting. They have
patted me with affirmation, folded my needs into prayers,
performed Herculean acts of service for everyone in our home, and
scrubbed small specks off my face with loving "spit baths."*

CAROL KENT

Sun pours through the kitchen window this spring
morning as I set my mother-in-law's hair. The plastic
box of curlers sits in front of her, the zippered case
with manicure essentials is to the left. At eighty-four, fingers
misshapen and stiff with arthritis, she can no longer perform
these rites of grooming.

"What would I do without you?" she says, as she always
does. "I would look so bad."

"Somebody else would if I couldn't," I reply as I eye her
upper lip and chin for pesky whiskers to tweeze. Her two daughters live a day-long drive away. Otherwise, they might be here,
doing this.

I move to her hands and swab away last week's pale pink polish. The nails on her right thumb and middle finger are jagged as a saw.

"Have you been trying to be a can opener again?" I chide. Childproof lids on her pain medicine are, well, a pain. She looks off, trying to appear angelic.

She twists the wedding ring set on her left hand back to position as I begin to file down the serrated nails. Her husband died eight years ago, but the ring has never come off.

"There will never be another Vernon," she often says in respect for their fifty-plus years together.

I remember him in better times, before Parkinson's disease finished ravaging his body. The diagnosis of the cruel disease came just as I gave birth to a little girl. My little boy was barely nineteen months old. I was thirty-seven and feeling my years as I struggled to keep up with a newborn and toddler.

Each day I managed to make it to bedtime still alive, though not kicking. But one day my "milk machine" rebelled, giving me an infection that left me feeling like I had the flu. Sick or not, baby still had to nurse and bigger brother had to be read to, played with, and fed. Oh yes, add in laundry and meals.

I knew I was in trouble. I'd been determined to be a self-sufficient mother, not a whiny one. But I'd reached the end of my sufficiency. I knew my solution was a phone call away. But I didn't want to bother them. *Bother* them, God prompted. *Let them help you.*

I dialed the number of my husband's parents.

"I'm sick," I said meekly. "Could you come help this afternoon?"

They lived a half-hour away. They were there in less than an hour. My need became their mission. Grandpa rocked the fussy baby, and Grandma washed the dishes and played with the toddler. I soaked my complaining anatomy in the bathtub for a while and then took a nap, confident that my helpers had everything under control.

When I woke up, they still weren't finished. They were giving my flowerbeds a fresh manicure.

Spring had prompted more than my front-yard roses to bloom. Dandelions, chickweed, red clover, and other intruders carpeted my rose bed. I had been too busy to take care of it, and it had bothered me.

"What would I do without you?" I said as I hugged them good-bye. It felt so good to get a break and have some of that nagging yard work done.

· ·

Now, two decades later, the roles are reversed. The one cared for has become the caregiver, and the caregiver, the one cared for. We mow her lawn, prune her roses, and trim her shrubs. But we can't keep Mother from weeding. There's enough determination in those knobby fingers to grab any weed.

"Nice day today," I remark as I put the last coat of rosy polish on her fingernails. "You wouldn't ruin this manicure with yard work, would you?"

She grins. "That's what gloves are for."

I know I can't stop her. And I won't.

"Beautiful as always," she says, fanning her fingers so the polish glistens in the sun.

She speaks wisdom without realizing it. Hands that serve are always beautiful. They weather well from the simple tasks of love.

* * *

Those who refresh others will themselves be refreshed.

PROVERBS 11:25 NLT

a treasure chest of memories

Cathy Gallagher

....

Memory is the treasury and guardian of all things.

CICERO

*H*er smile faded. Her expression turned wistful. Her eyes took on a faraway look as she stared into the distance. "Do you want to hear one of my most vivid memories?" she asked, her voice hesitant, serious, and soft.

"Of course I do," I said, not realizing I would see her differently afterward.

Mom and I had been enjoying a rare and wonderful mother-daughter moment, sipping coffee at the kitchen table. We had been digging up and dusting off memories — buried treasures — from the shelves of our minds that the other had either long forgotten or remembered differently. We held them up to each other like priceless jewels to be studied, admired, and put back for safekeeping. Our sharing had been laced with laughter, so her sudden mood change surprised me.

"I'm remembering a morning when you were little and your dad had been out of work for quite a while," Mom said. "Money was tight. We had enough to eat, but no extra servings. That morning, after our breakfast prayer, I poured you and your sister small glasses of orange juice. When you finished yours, you held up your glass and asked, 'More please?'"

"Oh, how I longed to give you more juice, but there wasn't enough. Feeling terrible, I said, 'Not today, but you may have more tomorrow.' Afterward I wondered, *Why didn't I give you more? What difference did it make if you drank the juice then or the next day?* To this day I feel awful about saying no."

When she finished, her eyes were brimming with tears; so were mine. *Perhaps I made her feel guilty that day,* I thought. "Oh, Mom, did I cry? What did I say or do after you said no?"

"Honey, you simply said, 'All right.'" I felt relieved.

As we talked her memory through, we explored how and why this memory of saying "no" had overshadowed all the times she had said "yes" and immediately given me a second serving. I assured Mom that saying "no" had *not* scarred me for life. I also saw her differently — not only as a mother but also as a woman with memories of experiences that either supported or crushed her dreams and desires.

Mom's memory was not about second servings, it was about symbols. To Mom, that second serving of orange juice symbolized her desire to give my sister and me the best of everything, whatever we asked, in abundance. Saying no caused her to feel like a failure in a role that was precious to her — being a mom. But she is not a failure. Mom is courageous, loving, and generous. She has always given my sister and me the best she had to offer.

My childhood memories are filled with loving moments: being quizzed by Mom on my times tables and Bible memory verses while doing the dishes together, curling up next to her while she read bedtime stories, filling baskets for the needy while she reminded me that there were people worse off than we were, countless times watching her bake chocolate chip cookies — enough for my sister and me to share with our friends. I also remember the times I asked for an extra serving and received it immediately.

As I shared these memories with Mom, her expression changed again; her smile was restored. Mom's anxiety over the past was replaced with the reminder that God has always met our needs. And he's still doing that today.

. . . .

So I tell you, don't worry about everyday life — whether you have enough food, drink, and clothes. Doesn't life consist of more than food and clothing? Look at the birds. They don't need to plant or harvest or put food in barns because your heavenly Father feeds them. And you are far more valuable to him than they are. Can all your worries add a single moment to your life? Of course not. . . . So don't worry about having enough food or drink or clothing. . . . Your heavenly Father already knows all your needs, and he will give you all you need from day to day if you live for him and make the Kingdom of God your primary concern. So don't worry about tomorrow, for tomorrow will bring its own worries. Today's trouble is enough for today.

MATTHEW 6:25–27, 31–34 NLT

"mama, i've got something to tell you"

Lucinda Secrest McDowell

· ·

Love that goes upward is worship; love that goes outward is affection; love that stoops is grace.

DONALD GRAY BARNHOUSE

ey, I'm a passionate person — a real Type A personality who, unfortunately, tends to *react* more than *respond* when caught in surprising and stressful situations. That reaction has often led me to apologize to my four children for my abrupt words and my "drama queen" antics.

As a Christian mom, I knew that I needed to learn to be less judgmental and more understanding, especially in my day-to-day mothering. I even understood that God's grace was offered to everyone and that it covered "a multitude of sins." In fact, in recent years God has been putting me through a real "Grace Tutorial" as he seeks to show me that his love for me is not based on my performance but simply because I belong to him.

Oh yeah, I *knew* all that, but one day God gave me an opportunity to show that my knowledge actually made a difference in my behavior.

. . . .

It was a snowy January afternoon in Connecticut, and I was frantically putting the finishing touches on a conference talk for an upcoming Boston event. As the words were flowing, it suddenly occurred to me that four-year-old Maggie had cooperated beautifully by staying quiet during her nap time. At that moment I heard a meek knock on the door and a little voice said, "Mama, I've got something to tell you."

"What is it, hon?" I absentmindedly queried while closing my notebook. I looked around to see the little person who went with the quiet voice.

Just then Maggie peered from around the door and exclaimed, "Mama, I cut off all my hair!"

And she had.

Her shoulder-length pageboy had been turned into a punk-like trim with several bangs only an eighth-inch long. For once in my life I was speechless. But in those first few seconds I heard a very clear voice inside my head, *"Careful, Cindy! She will always remember the way you handle this one!"*

I was at a crucial time in my life. God was teaching me about God's grace being a gift to us, one we don't deserve and can never earn. And now, while writing *about* grace, I was suddenly faced with the Lab Exam!

Maggie knew that what she had done was wrong, and she already showed signs of regret. Her questions poured out:

"Mama, can you make my hair long again?"

"Mama, am I still pretty?"

"Mama, do you still love me?"

So instead of my usual dramatic overreaction, I simply pulled her close for comfort and a hug. I knew that my "actions-have-consequences" sermon would have to wait. Maggie may have deserved punishment, but what she needed right then was assurance. So I washed her hair, trimmed it neatly, and told her that no matter what she did or what she looked like, I would always love her. For her, at that time, it was enough, and for me, it was encouraging to see that I could grow up in Christ.

When I have "blown it big time" and shuffled into the presence of God saying, "Lord, I have something to tell you . . . ," I come not only for confession but also to find that same assurance of God's love.

He never thunders out condemnation: "You jerk! I can't *believe* you did that again for the fifty-first time! Will you *never* learn? I'm outta here!"

Hardly. He stoops down to where I am and picks me up. Then he offers me what I don't deserve — his grace. And I crawl up into the lap of my heavenly Father and press into his loving embrace.

· ·

May our Lord Jesus Christ himself and God our Father,
who loved us and by his grace gave us eternal encouragement
and good hope, encourage your hearts and strengthen you
in every good deed and word.

2 Thessalonians 2:16–17

sharp shoes!

Diana Pintar

*The most important thing in communication
is to hear what isn't being said.*

PETER DRUCKER

ow! Sharp shoes, Vince!" Aunt Janis exclaimed.

Almost immediately, Vince started walkin' weird — with toes pointed outward in a duck-like waddle.

"Vince, do those new shoes hurt your feet?" I asked.

"No," he replied. "Aunt Janis told me I had sharp shoes, and I'm afraid they'll cut my legs."

It was the end of a long bare-footed summer. In anticipation of the upcoming school year, we purchased a pair of shiny brown loafers for Vince, our soon-to-enter-first-grade son. Aunt Janis intended that her words, *sharp shoes*, be received as a compliment, but Vince, then six, did not hear them in that way. Deaf until he was four, Vince had not yet learned the subtleties of the English language.

Vince was much like Amelia Bedelia, the fictional house-keeper with a literal mind. Like Amelia, who upset the household when she dressed the chicken and trimmed the steak with ribbons and lace, Vince heard in black and white. Casual conversation often upset him.

On another occasion, as we exited the church at the end of the service, our pastor greeted Vince with a seemingly innocent question: "Are you keeping your nose clean, Vince?"

Vince looked stricken and dashed to the restroom. Understanding how Vince heard (and often misunderstood) the intent of the words of others, I quickly followed.

The men's restroom was forbidden territory for women, even for mothers on rescue missions. I waited. Before long, Vince emerged, red-faced and angry.

"What's wrong with my nose?" he demanded.

"Nothing, Vince," I replied.

"Then why did Pastor Marv want to know if I was keeping it clean? Was he making fun of me?"

"No. That was just his way of saying 'Hi.'"

"Why didn't he just say 'Hi' then?" Vince sputtered. Try as hard as he might, Vince simply did not *get* idioms.

I hadn't really thought about the meaning of an idiom for quite a while. The dictionary defines this unique word as "a manner of speaking that is natural to native speakers of a language." For those in the know, idioms are a kind of verbal shorthand. For people like Vince (or Amelia Bedelia) they are a source of perplexity. Imagine how some familiar idioms must have sounded to my son:

- I have been *beating my brains out*.
- Don't get *bent out of shape*.
- My *eyes popped out* when I saw that.
- I finished by the *skin of my teeth*.
- I'm *pooped*.

We laugh at how Vince heard things in those days, but I've realized I'm often guilty of the same thing. Perhaps you've encountered a situation like I did:

I emerged from my bedroom after spending hours getting ready for a special evening with my husband. Presenting myself for final inspection (translated — "for wild applause and praise"), I asked my unsuspecting mate, "How do I look?"

"Fine," he responded.

That was not the word I was looking for. My husband, Mike, insists that *fine* means exactly what Webster's says it means, "superior in kind, quality, or appearance; excellent." Right! When I hear *fine*, I want to go back to my dressing room and start getting ready to go out all over again.

Words are funny, and I began to realize that sometimes as a mom and as a wife I hear things in a way that isn't that different from the way my son derives his meanings. Words have a way of morphing in meaning somewhere between the lips of the speaker and the ears of the hearer, confusing our verbal exchanges.

I'm realizing my mothering is better when I *listen with my heart* to the *heartbeat* of my children. It means I have to hear "what is *not* being said." That takes work, but I'm discovering it's worth it.

Communication in the best of circumstances is difficult. Between God and man it would be impossible — if God were not a communicator *par excellence*. I've taught my children that God sent his Son, Jesus Christ, the living Word (and, in a sense, a living idiom) to tell us how much he loves us. Jesus revealed the heart of God both *with* words and *without* words. My little boy with "sharp shoes" is grown now, and he fully understands that God expressed his love most clearly without words when he spread his arms on the Cross and died for us.

. . . .

Whoever has ears, let them hear.

Matthew 11:15 TNIV

conan, the barbarian prophet

Ellie Kay

···

*It is likely your boy possesses a measure of competitive and
adventuresome spirit. If you as a parent understand and respond to
this nature, both you and your son will be more in sync.*

DR. JAMES DOBSON, BRINGING UP BOYS

*J*oshua was eighteen months old when he got his nickname. The older kids knew they couldn't hit him
because he was the "baby," but they could sure run
away and scream. One day I heard a ruckus and found this
overly aggressive baby chasing all four of his siblings down the
hall, hitting them with a plastic sword. He had stripped down
to his diaper and, just as a cat will bring a dead mouse and place
it as his master's feet, Joshua was proud of his conquest. He
beamed with pride as he cornered all of his siblings on the
couch in front of Mom.

A couple months later, Joshua tried to jump from the top
bunkbed to the other set of bunkbeds across the room. He
didn't quite make it. He hit the edge of the bed with a thud. It
took eight stitches to put his lip back on.

Two months after that, we had just moved 3,000 miles and he fell into the corner of a trailer hitch — while chasing Bethany with a plastic cowboy gun. Our first stop for business in our new town was in the emergency room — we expected to be regulars. It took three stitches to mend that wound and he sports a scar on his forehead to this day.

When "Conan the Baby Barbarian" made a commitment to Christ at the age of six, his personality changed. He developed a zeal for God that would not be stifled.

We were at home eating dinner when Joshua asked Bob about his new job, getting directly to the point.

"Does your new boss, the general, know Jesus, Papa?"

Bob was surprised at the question and had to think about it a moment because he'd only been working for the general for a week,

"Well, no, he's a good man and great to work for, but I don't think he knows Jesus," Bob replied.

"Well," Joshua said in his typical, loud, future-general-like manner, "you gotta just tell him! You gotta walk into that office. Go up to his desk. And just *tell* him about Jesus!"

. . . .

The next Sunday, we were eating lunch when Joshua asked seven-year-old Jonathan, "Did you know that we are the salt of the earth?"

Jonathan shrugged his shoulders because Joshua had been "preaching" to him all weekend. "Yeah, so what?"

"Well, that means we need to be good to be salt." Joshua put down the salt shaker and picked up the other shaker. "I guess the bad people are the pepper."

The mailman was making his rounds one day and Joshua was playing in the front yard. As the mailman put the mail in the box, Joshua walked up to him with purposeful strides. "Hi, Mr. Mailman, you know your way around the neighborhood, but do you know your way to heaven?"

Yet another time we were in "Super Stuff Mart" buying more (you guessed it) stuff. When it was our turn at the register, Joshua looked at the cashier and asked, "Hi there, lady. You got a lot of money in that register, but did you know you cannot buy your way into heaven?"

And recently, we went into a video rental store to pick up a copy of *The Rookie*. As we passed by the "comedy" section, Joshua caught a glimpse of some inappropriate covers on some videos. The clerk was checking our rentals when Joshua announced, "You know, mister, there are some nasty-looking covers there on those videos you sell. What do you think Jesus thinks about them?"

As a little boy, Conan needs our influence to temper his zeal for Christ with wisdom.

Maybe we all could stand to have a little more Conan in us and be less fearful in sharing our faith. If we trust God to give us the words and the opportunities, we can share his love with a needy world with all the confidence of a conqueror. But I recommend you leave the plastic sword at home.

. . . .

No, in all these things we are more than conquerors
through him who loved us.

ROMANS 8:37

who do you love?

Ellie Kay

. . . .

It has hands to help others, feet to hasten to the poor and needy,
eyes to see misery and want, ears to hear the sighs and sorrows of
men. That is what love looks like.

AUGUSTINE

*J*onathan, please go put these swim goggles with all the
rest." Bob handed his son the goggles as he continued
cleaning up the clutter in the living room.

Much later, Jonathan came up to Bob and gave him a spon-
taneous hug and kiss and threw in an "I love you, Papa!"

"I love you too, Jonathan," Bob said as he returned the hug.
Then he remembered the goggles. "Hey, where did you put
those goggles I gave you?"

"You told me to put them with the rest of the goggles, so I
threw them in the pool." With that, he scurried off to play with
his baseball cards.

Our kids will oftentimes take us literally, so we have to be
careful in the words we use when we joke around with them.

We especially need to be quite literal in how we tell them we love them. In other words, we need to say it.

In our home we've had a game we've played with our kids since they were babies. When they were little, we'd rock them in our laps and ask, "Who loves you?" then we'd answer the question with "Mama loves you," followed with tickles and hugs and kisses. Sometimes we'd ask, "Who do you love?" to get them in the habit of verbally returning that affirmation.

Parents sometimes try to spell love in gifts, vacations, privileges, and even cash, and there's nothing wrong with that in moderation. But verbal and physical affirmations are far more important than material alternatives when it comes to saying "I love you."

Even now, as my children range in age from twenty-three down to eight, I will still occasionally ask, "Who do you love?" to remind them of how much they are loved and how they have the freedom to love in return.

But the greatest example of love that a mom can point her children to is the love of a perfect God who sent his Son to die for the imperfect. I'm so glad God stands in my gap as a parent. He loves me so much that he's the God of second, third, and fourth chances. I entered into a relationship with him as a seven-year-old and that genuine relationship took me through a turbulent childhood, carried me beyond an abusive relationship as a young adult, and has brought me through the unique stress of being married to a husband who often flies into harm's way. But more important, God has taken the pains and sorrows of the past and given victory over victimization to help me be the kind of mom my kids need. They know their mom isn't perfect, but they also know she loves them.

No matter where you are as a mom, you can imagine God asking you, "Who loves you?" as he takes delight in everything about you. If you take the time to listen, you can hear his voice — in creation, in your children, in everything around you — asking, "Who do *you* love?"

....

For God so loved the world that he gave his one and only Son, that whoever believes in him shall not perish but have eternal life.

JOHN 3:16

a treasured letter

Carol Kent

....

I sat down on the couch and ran my fingers around the string of forty-eight faux pearls (my mother's pearls). And as I did, those small, smooth gems became for me, touchstones — linking me to the memories of a godly woman who lived her simple life in a way that witnessed God's glory.

DAISY HEPBURN, FORGET NOT HIS BLESSINGS

*M*y wedding day was fast approaching and I could feel anxiety rising within my heart:

Am I making the biggest mistake of my life?

Is this really the man I should spend the rest of my life with?

Are we rushing into this marriage? (We had already dated for four years.)

Do I really know what love is?

Can a woman ever be sure that the man she is marrying is really right for her?

Could I do more for God in my lifetime if I stayed single?

I thought I was in love with Gene, but I didn't want to get married and be sorry later. I wished for a neon sign in the sky from God that said: MARRY THIS MAN! YOU WON'T REGRET IT! HE'S MY CHOICE FOR YOU! That sign never appeared, but God used my mother to deliver a calming message to my heart.

Mother was very busy with getting my four younger sisters and my brother ready for the big celebration, so I was extremely surprised when she handed me a letter on the day before my wedding. It wasn't on fancy embossed stationery, but I instinctively knew *this* letter would become one of my most treasured possessions. I read:

Dear Carol,

I feel very close to you tonight. I just want to write my thoughts about you down on paper. I'm remembering how I longed for a child of my own. Even before I was married, I dreamed of the day when I'd have a little girl of my own. I'll never forget the day I found out I was going to have you. I was very close to the Lord at that time. I talked to Him often about the child He would commit to my keeping. Before you were ever born you were dedicated to my Lord Jesus Christ.

When you arrived, they told me I had a baby girl with red fuzzy hair, weighing 5 lb. 14 oz., 21 inches long. I was too thrilled for words! My first thought was, "Is she normal?" My second thought was, "Thank you, Lord, for my own little baby girl." I could hardly believe it could be possible. Me with a little baby girl. How good God was to me!

I whispered to you and talked to you and told you again and again about Jesus right from the start. As you grew older, you'd smile as though you really understood what I was saying.

Time passed and then came your first day of school, piano lessons for which you hated to practice, and finally that day on the farm when we sat listening to the radio program, "Unshackled." When it was over you were crying and told me you were such a sinner. There on our knees that tremendous transaction was made and you were born again into God's family.

You were growing up so fast, and we had many precious times of prayer together. Then came your first date, and eventually Gene entered your life as a boyfriend. His interest in spiritual things and his hunger for the Word of God made me love him very soon. Then you were off to college and the next four years of your life seemed to fly by.

I was so happy when you became engaged to Gene. I think I loved him long before you did. Now the time for your marriage has arrived. This is your last night in our home as my little Carol Joy Afman. Soon you'll be a married woman. I face this night with mixed emotions. I'm so happy for you both, but there will be an empty place here. Always remember how much I love you.

May God's richest blessings be yours. Always put Him first. Pray much about your relationship to one another before God. Don't neglect spending time together in the Bible — and you just have to be the happiest married couple this side of heaven.

Love and Prayers,
Mother[*]

I read the letter twice, carefully folded it, and placed it in my Bible. I felt a quiet confidence emerge within my spirit. Gene *was* the right man for me. Our relationship had been covered with prayer from the very beginning. We shared common interests and had big dreams about what we wanted to do for God in this lifetime.

That day my uncertainty was replaced with confidence. God used my Mother's letter to confirm what I had known all along. Mother had also reminded me of my early commitment to Christ, her continuing prayers for my future, and of her deep love for me as her daughter.

The following day I walked down the aisle into the waiting arms of my groom, knowing I was making the right choice.

* * * * *

I will instruct you and teach you in the way you should go;
I will counsel you and watch over you.

PSALM 32:8

---

* This letter originally appeared in *Mothers Have Angel Wings* by Carol Kent, copyright © 1997. Used by permission of NavPress, *www.navpress.com*. All rights reserved.

loser mom

Ellie Kay

I don't need eyeglasses, but I'm a sucker for a trendy
pair of sunglasses. The only problem is that I always
lose them, scratch them, or break them. I remember getting an expensive pair of Ray-Bans for Mother's Day one
year that I lost before Memorial Day. Another time, I got a pair
of Oakleys that I wore to the lake. They blew off my head the
first time I was out in the boat. In New York City, I decided I
needed some pricey Vuarnet glasses that I wore on the Staten
Island Ferry. They're in the water.

Then there was the pair of Foster Grants that cost only $4
on clearance and lasted me five years. It seems the less I spend
on glasses, the longer I keep them. Sunglasses are an important
commodity for moms. If moms didn't wear sunglasses, we'd all

have crow's feet by the time we were thirty and have to have plastic surgery by the time we're forty. You can tell a lot about a person by the kind of glasses they wear. Christian moms wear several types that help them handle the roles they play in family life.

For example, when I put on my glasses with the rhinestone-studded cross in the corner, I'm the Spiritual Powerhouse Mom — ready to go to Bible study, teach a class, volunteer at church, and lead my children in prayer over lost term reports or school yard bullies. When I put on my Taxi Driver glasses, I'm ready to shuttle five kids to thirteen activities in a single day. By slapping on a pair of protective goggles, I'm the Fitness Queen, ready to play racquetball and keep fit. My Chef Shades keep those grease splatters away when I'm the Skilled Chef, preparing my family's nutritionally sound meals. Those rainbow-tinted glasses transform a mere mortal into Tightwad Wizard Mom who never overspends at Stuff Mart and always pays her bills on time.

Then there's the pair of Looney Tunes glasses that I wear as the Chief Entertainer who can throw an amazingly creative birthday party or organize numerous field trips to zoos, parks, and museums. My "Men in Black" glasses send the message that I'm out to protect my kids from strangers, Internet porn, TV shock, and video game violence.

There's only one problem with all these glasses — I tend to lose 'em, scratch 'em, or break 'em. Yep, there are times when

I can't win when it comes to keeping up with all that's required in my "mommy glasses."

But you know what? God understands. He created me knowing that I would put tons of pressure on myself to be the be-all and end-all for all of my children. And he knew that I would "lose it" on occasion. That's why he created grace. God doesn't require me to be perfect, only that I persevere. God knows that moms are going to lose a pair of glasses here and there, and when we are fumbling in the dark, all he asks is that we reach out for his hand. What a relief.

He's even given me a special pair of spiritual rose-colored glasses that help me choose to be grateful for what I have instead of longing for what I do not have. They protect me from the glare of self-criticism and help me find my way again when I've gotten off track. These are priceless shades that never scratch and never get lost. Wanna try on a pair?

. . . .

Keep me as the apple of your eye;
hide me in the shadow of your wings.

PSALM 17:8

fast-food prayers

Ellie Kay

. . . .

Minister: "So your mother says your prayers for you each night. What does she say?" The youngster replied, "Thank God he's in bed."

CHARLES SWINDOLL

*P*rayer can become rote if we're not careful. Even if we don't have a standard prayer for meals or bedtime, such as "Now I lay me down to sleep, I pray the Lord my soul to keep ..." we can still find ourselves uttering the same prayers again and again.

Our oldest son, Daniel, works in a fast-food restaurant on weekends. He was recently working the drive-through. When the bell rings to indicate a customer is at the speaker box, he is supposed to say, "Welcome to Dairy Queen, please order when you are ready." On busy days, he repeats this phrase dozens of times every hour — it's second nature to him. But on one particular day, he was about to go on his lunch break and was daydreaming about the burger, fries, and shake that would soon be in his grasp and down his hungry hatch. When the drive-through bell rang, Daniel, à la Pavlov's dog, leaned into the microphone and announced:

"Thank you, Jesus, for this food."

. . . .

My poor son was very embarrassed.

But hidden within his embarrassment is a great lesson for all of us. How many times do we get in the habit of saying the same prayers, singing the same songs in church, and lose the meaning of the words in the process?

It's also a reminder that we can treat God as we do a fast-food employee — expecting him to get us our answers in two minutes or we'll get angry at the Almighty's lack of a response.

My husband is a great example to our kids in the prayer department, although it wasn't that way at first. When we were newly married, Bob told me that he was intimidated to pray in front of me. It took him years to feel confident praying out loud. Moms need to be aware that a lot of dads feel the same way, and they need to give their husbands room to grow in confidence.

Bob now prays frequently in front of our family and others. For example, when our house is in chaos and the whole family seems to be in an argumentative mood, he just blurts out loud, "Dear Jesus, I am sorry for my contribution to this lack of peace in our home. I pray that you would restore peace and harmony in this home and rebuke the enemy." And guess what. It works!

My sons are following their father's example. Not just at Dairy Queen, either. The other day, I heard thirteen-year-old Philip fighting with eight-year-old Joshua over a video game. Philip stopped, took his brother's hand, and said, "Dear Jesus, please help us stop arguing and please make us live together in peace." The scene warmed my heart, and I'm sure it did the same for God. If you find that your prayer life has become too routine, just remember that the prayers that are sure to get God's attention are the ones that come straight from the heart.

* * *

Therefore confess your sins to each other and pray for each other so that you may be healed. The prayer of a righteous person is powerful and effective.

JAMES 5:16 TNIV

About Carol Kent, General Editor

Carol Kent is a popular international public speaker best known for being dynamic, humorous, encouraging, and biblical. She is a former radio show cohost and has been a guest on numerous television and radio programs. She is the president of Speak Up Speaker Services, a Christian speakers' bureau, and the founder and director of Speak Up With Confidence seminars, a ministry committed to helping Christians develop their communication skills. She has also founded the nonprofit organization Speak Up for Hope, which benefits the families of incarcerated individuals. A member of the National Speakers Association, Carol is often scheduled more than a year in advance for keynote addresses at conferences and retreats throughout the United States and abroad.

She holds a master's degree in communication arts and a bachelor's degree in speech education. Her books include: *When I Lay My Isaac Down, Becoming a Woman of Influence, Mothers Have Angel Wings, Secret Longings of the Heart, Tame Your Fears, Speak Up With Confidence*, and *Detours, Tow Trucks, and Angels in Disguise*. She has also cowritten with Karen Lee-Thorp *My Soul's Journey* and the *Designed for Influence Bible Studies*. Carol has been featured on the cover of *Today's Christian Woman* and her articles have been published in a wide variety of magazines. To schedule Carol to speak for your event, call 888-870-7719 or contact her at *www.SpeakUp SpeakerServices.com* or *www.CarolKent.org*.

About Ellie Kay

Ellie Kay is the mother of seven children and the wife of a former military fighter pilot who is now a corporate test pilot. She is a graduate of Colorado Christian University and is trademarked as America's Family Financial Expert®. As a regular guest on numerous national television shows, her appearances include CNBC's *Power Lunch*, the Fox Network's *Fox and Friends*, and CNNfn's *The Flip Side*. Her fun and witty radio commentary for *Money Matters* is heard on more than five hundred media markets internationally. As the author of eight books, her titles include the best-selling book *Shop, Save and Share* as well as *Heroes at Home*, a Gold Medallion Book Award finalist. She has contributed expertise to such periodicals as *Reader's Digest*, *Woman's Day*, *Woman's World*, *Redbook*, *Budget Living*, *Today's Christian Woman*, *Focus on the Family*, *Marriage Partnership*, and *HomeLife*.

As a national speaker, she enjoys making audiences laugh while communicating practical information. In her free time, she is a corporate consultant who has been described by a *Reader's Digest* writer as "the gateway to middle America." In this capacity, she has served as an advocate for the American family's finances in her work as a spokesperson for Entertainment.com, Mastercard, eHealthInsurance.com, and Visa Providian. For information on Ellie's schedule, go to www.elliekay.com.

Contributors

Charlotte Adelsperger is an author and speaker who has written for numerous publications, including *Focus on the Family, Clubhouse, Woman's World, Stories for the Heart,* and *Chicken Soup for the Soul.* Charlotte is a popular speaker at women's events and writers' conferences. Contact her 913-345-1678 or author04@aol.com.

Pauline Afman is the mother of Carol Kent, four more daughters, and a son. A master storyteller, she has been entertaining and encouraging her family and other audiences for much of her adult life. Pauline lives in Fremont, Michigan, and can be reached at: cp afman@ncats.net.

Sandi Banks' book *Anchors of Hope: Finding Peace Amidst the Storms of Life* offers hope to a hurting world. Her speaking will warm your heart, tickle your funny bone, and refresh your spirit. Sandi is director of Adult Worldview Conferences for Summit Ministries and served on the ACTS International board of directors. For information, contact Sandi at *www.anchorsofhope.com* or sandi@anchors ofhope.com.

Joy Carlson is Carol Kent's sister. She's a pastor's wife who strives to bring creative arts into the worship experience. She also writes and directs dramas and monologues. As the mother of seven children, her experience with family and ministry has equipped her to encourage women in matters of faith and obedience. Contact Joy at 888-870-7719 or at joybells@riverview.net

Annetta E. Dellinger is known as "The Joy Lady." She is founder and president of Joyful Ministries and a speaker with Speak Up

Speaker Services. She is author of thirty books, including *Be Joyful . . . Who Me? Mini Joy-Spirations to Energize Your Day*. For information, contact Annetta at www.Annettadellinger.com. To schedule Annetta for a speaking engagement, call 888-870-7719.

Anne Denmark delights in using her spiritual gift of encouragement. Anne has a master's degree in adult education and a bachelor's degree in child development, with continuing education in floral design and clowning. She is a staff trainer with Speak Up With Confidence seminars, and her stories appear in *Mothers Have Angel Wings* and *Tame Your Fears*. Together with her husband, Don, she trains leaders of young married couples.

Bonnie Afman Emmorey is Carol Kent's sister. She is a speaker consultant with Speak Up Speaker Services, teaches communication skills at Speak Up With Confidence seminars, and is helping to launch Speak Up for Hope. For information, go to *www.SpeakUp ForHope.org* and *www.SpeakUpSpeakerServices.com*.

Rozanne Frazee married her high school sweetheart and has been a pastor's wife for fifteen years. She is the mother of one daughter and three sons who are the delight of her life. She is the cofounder of a national organization for mothers of young children called Creative Homemakers. She is an interpreter for the deaf and loves to run, play tennis, and read. You can contact her at rozanne@pantego.org.

Cathy Gallagher has been a salesperson, marketing manager, customer service director, assistant dean, and president of her own speaking and writing business. She has authored numerous articles for business and was the ghostwriter of a book on business communications. She is actively involved in a prayer ministry and a prison ministry through her church. Cathy speaks and writes on a wide variety of subjects. Contact Cathy to speak for your group by calling 888-870-7719.

Jill Lynnele Gregory lives in the metro-Detroit, Michigan, area with her husband and four children. Jill keeps busy with her children, including a special-needs child, and with her involvement in women's ministries at her church. Contact her at gregoryfam@wideopen west.com.

Jolanta Hoffmann is a music educator and pastor's wife who loves to direct children's choirs, dramas, and musicals. She is also involved in the adult music ministry at her church as a guitarist for the praise team, and as a mezzo-soprano soloist. She lives with her husband, three children, and a variety of pets adopted by the children.

Shirley Carter Liechty works as an administrative assistant for speaker and author Carol Kent. She serves on the women's ministry team of her church and speaks at women's events on spiritual growth, hope after depression, and grandparenting. Her hobbies are gardening, writing, and photographing her grandchildren. Contact Shirley at sliechty@myexcel.com.

Lucinda Secrest McDowell, a graduate of Gordon-Conwell Seminary, is an international conference speaker and author *What We've Learned So Far, Amazed by Grace, Quilts from Heaven, A Southern-Style Christmas*, and *Women's Spiritual Passages*. She enjoys giving innovative presentations through her ministry, "Encouraging Words that Transform!" Contact her at *www.EncouragingWords.net* or at cindy@encouragingwords.net.

Diana Pintar is president of The Next Step Ministries, Inc., and travels nationally as a speaker for women's conferences and retreats. Diana is a speaker/trainer with Speak Up With Confidence seminars.

For additional information, visit her website at *www.TheNextStep Online.com*. To schedule Diana as a speaker, call 888-870-7719.

Allison L. Shaw is a freelance writer and editor from Sacramento, California. She is passionate about children's literature, her career as a librarian, and her husband, Michael. Her published work appears in the *Sacramento Bee*, several anthologies, and pages scattered throughout the World Wide Web. To contact Allison, write to allie_shaw@hotmail.com or call 916-366-3021.

Carol Van Atta has been set free from a number of past bondages and addictions. She is the founder of a ministry for women, Becoming a Warrior for Christ. Her heartfelt desire is to help women find freedom and wholeness in their relationships with each other and with Jesus Christ. She is the author of *Slaying the Shadows — Book One: The Defender of our Souls*, a spiritual thriller with eternal implications. She speaks to women's groups and writes for a number of publications, including *Christian Women Today*, *Look UP* magazine, *Hearts at Home* magazine, and *Proverbs 31 Women*. For speaking and ministry information, visit Carol at www.carolvanatta.com.

Jeanne Zornes is a women's retreat and conference speaker, and a writer of hundreds of articles and seven books, including *When I Prayed for Patience . . . God Let Me Have It!* She lives in Washington State. Contact her at P.O. Box 4362, Wenatchee, WA 98807-4392.

kisses of sunshine

Hardcover
0-310-24766-7

Hardcover
0-310-24846-9

Hardcover
0-310-24765-9

Hardcover
0-310-24767-5

Hardcover
0-310-24768-3

Pick up a copy today at your favorite bookstore!

ZONDERVAN™

GRAND RAPIDS, MICHIGAN 49530 USA

WWW.ZONDERVAN.COM

We want to hear from you. Please send your comments about this book to us in care of zreview@zondervan.com. Thank you.

GRAND RAPIDS, MICHIGAN 49530 USA

WWW.ZONDERVAN.COM